THE SUGAR BLOCKERS DIET™

COOKBOOK

More Than 170 Recipes
to Lose Weight,
Lower Blood Sugar Spikes,
and Beat Diabetes

THE EDITORS OF **Prevention**®
WITH ROB THOMPSON, MD

RODALE

© 2012 by Rodale Inc.
Photographs © 2012 by Rodale Inc.

Printed in the United States of America

Rodale Inc. makes every effort to use acid-free ♾, recycled paper ♻.

Photographs by Mitch Mandel/Rodale Inc.

Book design by Toby Fox

Library of Congress Cataloging-in-Publication Data

Thompson, Rob, 1945-
The sugar blockers diet cookbook : more than 170 recipes to lose weight, lower blood
sugar spikes, and beat diabetes / the editors of Prevention; with Rob Thompson.
p.   cm.
Includes index.
ISBN 978-1-60961-759-2 direct hardcover
1. Reducing diets—Recipes.   2. Non-insulin-dependent diabetes—Diet therapy—Recipes.
3. Glycemic index.   4. Weight loss.   5. Cookbooks.   I. Prevention Magazine Health Books.
II. Title.
RM222.2.T4849   2012
613.2'833—dc23   2011045958

2   4   6   8   10   9   7   5   3   hardcover

We inspire and enable people to improve their lives and the world around them.

For more of our products, visit **prevention.com** or call 800-848-4735.

CONTENTS

INTRODUCTION

———●

You want to lose weight. You *need* to manage your diabetes better (or perhaps your doctor has diagnosed you with prediabetes, metabolic syndrome, or other risk factors). To do that, you think you have to give up all the foods you love—pizza, pasta, chocolate, the occasional cupcake—and you're not sure you can bear to.

Happily, you don't have to.

In fact, how would you like to start your day with an Italian Omelet, French Toast with Sour Cream and Walnuts, or Nutty Granola?

Sound good? Then perhaps you'd like to lunch on a classic Open-Faced Steak Sandwich or Mushroom Turkey Burger. Or how about a hearty Orange-Jicama Chicken Salad?

Still interested? Well, how about a predinner snack, too—Smoked Salmon Dip, perhaps, or Spicy Mexican Peanuts or Cheddar-Bacon Crackers? Then, on to the main course: Herb-Crusted Steak with Potato Fries, Asian Pork Burgers, or Chicken Paprikash.

But there's *more:* dessert! Make your choice: Fresh Fruit Tart, Key Lime Pie, or decadent Cherries 'n' Chocolate Sundaes.

How can you enjoy all of these rich and delectable foods while still losing weight and balancing your blood sugar? It's simple: All you have to do is block sugar.

As editors at *Prevention* magazine, the nation's #1 healthy living brand, we hear a lot of different theories about how to shed the pounds—and most of the time, we find that when a weight loss plan sounds too good to be true, we're right to be skeptical. So when we first learned about sugar blockers from Rob Thompson, MD, a preventive cardiologist who has treated hundreds of patients with diabetes, obesity, and heart disease, we challenged him to help us put his plan to the test. As described in his new book, *The Sugar Blockers Diet,* we assembled a test panel of 16 men and women to try it—and we were astonished by the results! As these people discovered, on the Sugar Blockers Diet, all you need to do to lose weight and prevent or treat prediabetes or diabetes is take a few simple actions:

▶ Identify those foods that lead to "sugar shocks"—spikes in blood sugar that occur immediately after meals.

▶ Avoid or limit them when you can.

▶ Block them when you can't.

As you'll see, this simple plan actually allows you to eat more tasty and satisfying food than you probably ever have—the recipes that follow prove it. And it can do great things not just for your weight but also for the quality of your life.

You can still eat carbs; you just have to either avoid those carbohydrates that cause sugar shocks or use sugar-blocking foods and techniques to outsmart their effects. That's easier than you think, and tastier than you'd imagine.

It all hinges on natural substances, found in many foods, that interfere with the breakdown of carbohydrates into sugar in your digestive tract and slow its absorption into your bloodstream. Not only do these natural sugar-blocking substances inhibit your body's absorption of sugar in the foods that contain them, but they can also block your body's absorption of sugar in other foods that you eat with these substances. That means you don't have to avoid carbs such as bread, potatoes, and rice completely—if you eat them with foods that contain sugar blockers, including many fruits and veggies, protein, nuts, cheese, vinegar, and even alcohol.

But there's even more you can do to lessen after-meal sugar spikes. The order in which you eat foods, your activities before and after you eat, how much fluid you drink with your meal, the time of day, even the amount of sleep you get—all affect how high your blood sugar goes after you eat a carbohydrate.

Along with the mouthwatering recipes in this book, the simple sugar-blocking tactics offered in the next few chapters not only will help you peel off those extra pounds but also will significantly—perhaps dramatically—benefit your health. Best of all, you'll see that they fit easily into your usual habits and lifestyle. For example, you'll learn about:

▶ The most abundant natural sugar blocker there is—and how to maximize its power

▶ The easiest ways to activate your body's own sugar-blocking systems

▶ The revolutionary new sugar-blocking medications that slow the entry of sugar into your bloodstream, reduce your body's needs for insulin, and reliably produce significant and lasting weight loss

On the Sugar Blockers Diet, you won't count calories, grams of carbohydrates, or grams of fat. You won't suffer through tiny portions of unappetizing foods. Like our test panelists, you *will* be amazed by the satisfying amounts of delicious foods you'll enjoy—and by a loss of up to 18½ pounds in 6 weeks.

The sugar-blocking methods described in this book have been proved to work. There's research to support them, and real people whose waistlines show the benefits of this simple, delicious way of eating. You'll find some of their stories in the next few chapters.

These people—with real lives and real health issues—didn't even try to reduce the amount of food they ate. They experienced neither gnawing hunger nor deprivation. Their results were impressive—and it wasn't just the numbers on the scale that improved. Most of our panelists also saw their blood sugar levels, blood pressure, and triglyceride levels come down—including one panelist who saw his triglycerides drop by an incredible 500 points. Many reported that their moods stabilized, and they found energy to spare as they enjoyed some of their favorite foods.

Although sugar blockers can't completely prevent the rise in blood sugar and in insulin demands that occurs after you eat sugar-shocking starchy carbs, they *can* reduce it significantly. And it doesn't take much sugar blocking to provide significant benefits. Reducing the size of after-meal blood sugar spikes by just 30 percent has been found to reduce insulin demands, promote weight loss, and make diabetes easier to control; it can also actually reverse prediabetes. Most remarkable, recent studies have discovered significant reductions in the incidence of heart disease among followers of low–glycemic load diets as well as people who take pharmaceutical sugar blockers.

On the Sugar Blockers Diet, you'll enjoy the foods you love as you drop pounds, reverse prediabetes or get your diabetes under control, normalize your blood pressure and cholesterol levels, and reduce your risk of heart disease and stroke. So get ready to eat hearty, get healthy—and, for perhaps the first time, stay slim for good!

WHAT
SUGAR BLOCKING
CAN DO FOR YOU

COMEDIAN JACKIE GLEASON, who played portly Ralph Kramden in the classic sitcom *The Honeymooners*, once said, "The second day of a diet is always easier than the first. By the second day, you're off it." Gleason's wry observation is funny because it's true. Food: You can't live with it, you can't live without it.

Get ready to be set free! The truth is, all you have to do to drop the pounds is *block sugar*. That's shorthand for slowing the breakdown of carbohydrates to sugar (glucose) in your digestive tract so that glucose enters your bloodstream slowly rather than all at once. That might seem like a simple thing, but it can produce powerful benefits for your weight and health.

And yes, it's easy, too.

Before we get into how sugar blockers work, there are a few facts you need to know about how your body converts the food you eat into energy.

Food contains three major nutrients: fats, proteins, and carbohydrates. Each nutrient has its own building block. Fats are made of fatty acids, proteins consist of amino acids, and carbohydrates are made of sugars such as glucose and fructose. Fat and protein come primarily from animal products such as eggs, meat, dairy products, and oily foods like nuts and olives. You get carbohydrates from plant products, including fruits, vegetables, flour products, potatoes, rice, and sugar. Your digestive tract has to break down each type of food to its basic building block—fatty acid, amino acid, or sugar—before it can be absorbed into your bloodstream.

Now let's start at the beginning—10,000 years ago.

● THE DISCOVERY OF STARCH

At the dawn of human history, man, as the expression goes, "ate clean." Along with meat, he consumed grasses, roots, and wild fruit. This vitamin-rich vegetation contained plenty of indigestible fiber and other substances that slow the speed at which carbohydrates break down to glucose. As a result of this roughage-filled diet, the digestive tracts of our prehistoric kin had to work hard to wrestle any "fuel"—that is, glucose—from plants. Most of the plant foods passed through their systems undigested, and whatever glucose they absorbed trickled, rather than rushed, into their bloodstreams.

About 10,000 years ago, this meat-and-veggie diet underwent a dramatic change: Humans discovered how to make food out of wild wheat and barley, which grew in abundance in regions that are now parts of Iraq and Syria. The seeds of these grasses are packed with starch, a powdery substance that consists of glucose molecules linked together in long chains. Enzymes in seeds can break the bonds that hold the starch molecules together and use the glucose for the energy needed to sprout.

Mother Nature intended starch to be used as an energy source for plants, not animals. To make sure predators couldn't get at the starch in these seeds, she encased them in rock-hard husks. However, some resourceful ancestors of ours learned to grind wheat and barley seeds between rocks and let the wind blow away the chaff. They had hit pay dirt: a huge, previously untapped source of easily digestible calories that could be stored between growing seasons and provide food year-round. Similar "refinement" of rice and millet, corn, and the potato—also packed with starch—followed.

It didn't take long for our ancestors to learn that refined carbohydrates could feed more people more dependably and easily than any other kind of food. Indeed, we modern humans now consume *hundreds of times* more starch than our forebears did. Starches now provide most of the calories for most of the people in the world.

With Civilization Come New Diseases

With the advent of agriculture, our prehistoric kin no longer had to be constantly on the move searching for food. Once humans learned to plant crops, they settled down and began to form communities—and, eventually, the start of civilization as we know it today. The cultivation of starches fostered agricultural societies that eventually came to dominate the world.

But there was a price to pay for our progress. The digestive systems of all animals are designed to handle diets specific to each species. When we humans gave up the hunter-gatherer lifestyle we were designed for and began to consume refined carbohydrates, we became shorter, less muscular, and prone to what scientists call diseases of civilization, including obesity, diabetes, and heart disease.

What was it about the change in diet that made us subject to these problems? It's not that humans had never eaten carbohydrates before. Some of our *really* ancient ancestors—apes and monkeys—lived on vegetation. The difference is that the plant parts we consume have become increasingly refined—stripped of their natural barriers to digestion. The rates of obesity, diabetes, and heart disease correlate directly with the lack of inhibitors to carbohydrate absorption in our diets. Today, Americans who consume below-average amounts of natural sugar-blocking substances have significantly higher rates of obesity, diabetes, and heart disease than do those who consume larger amounts. Why does stripping plants of their natural barriers to digestion make us prone to these health threats?

It has to do with the hormone insulin.

● INSULIN RESISTANCE AND "DIABESITY"

While researchers and health experts are now regularly sounding the alarm about weight gain, it wasn't long ago that obesity was all but ignored as a medical problem. However, doctors have always taken diabetes seriously. They couldn't help noticing that the skyrocketing obesity of the last 30 years was accompanied by a virtual epidemic of type 2 diabetes. Indeed, research has since shown that type 2 diabetes and obesity are just different manifestations of the same disease process. In fact, this process now has its own name: *diabesity*. And if you understand what brings on this kind of diabetes, you'll also see why so many people these days are overweight.

If you have diabetes, your body has lost its ability to maintain normal blood sugar levels. (Keep in mind that when doctors refer to blood "sugar," they are talking about levels of the sugar glucose in the bloodstream.) It's important to understand that there are two distinct kinds of diabetes: type 1 and type 2. Type 1 diabetes, also called juvenile diabetes, typically strikes children and young adults. It's caused by damage to the beta cells of the pancreas, which make the hormone insulin. This damage to beta cells is caused by an immune reaction to an infection.

One of insulin's jobs is to transport sugar out of your blood and into your cells, where it is either stored as fat or used for energy. Because of damage to their beta cells, people with type 1 diabetes don't make enough insulin, so sugar backs up in their bloodstream. For people with type 1 diabetes, high blood sugar is purely the result of a lack of insulin. Otherwise, the body chemistry functions normally.

In the past, children and young people with type 1 diabetes often died for lack of insulin. Insulin shots, introduced in the 1920s, were a godsend for these people, allowing them to live normal lives.

By contrast, people with type 2 diabetes, also known as adult-onset diabetes, often don't need insulin to control their blood sugar. Doctors used to think that type 2 diabetes was just a milder form of type 1—also caused by a lack of insulin, but just not as severe a deficiency. Then, in the 1980s, scientists discovered that the beta cells of patients with type 2 diabetes actually make *plenty* of insulin. The problem is that their bodies lose sensitivity to it, a condition called insulin resistance. Consequently, the beta cells have to make more-than-normal amounts of insulin to compensate for the body's loss of sensitivity to it.

MUSCLE UP Against Diabetes

INSULIN RESISTANCE isn't caused by a malfunction of some organ inside your body, like your liver, kidneys, or spleen. *It's a muscle problem.* Muscles are glucose gobblers, and the target of most of the insulin your body produces. Insulin resistance means that your muscles have lost sensitivity to this important hormone. The reason? *You don't use them enough.*

The only real cure for insulin resistance, then, is to use your muscles. Physical activity—walking, swimming, cycling, gardening—can turn the vicious cycle of insulin resistance into a virtuous cycle. Activating your muscles restores insulin sensitivity, which lowers insulin levels, which promotes weight loss, which further increases insulin sensitivity.

The good news is that you don't have to engage in grueling workouts to start this virtuous cycle. As you'll see in Chapter 3, all you have to do to sensitize your muscles to insulin, lose weight, and prevent or better control your diabetes is walk for as little as 20 minutes a day.

Lose Insulin Sensitivity, Gain Weight

Remember, your body doesn't need much insulin to handle fat and protein. You mainly need insulin to metabolize carbohydrates—foods your digestive tract turns to sugar. If you have insulin resistance, your beta cells have to pump out more and more insulin—up to six times normal amounts, in fact—to process the carbohydrates you consume.

Insulin resistance goes on for years before diabetes occurs. Insulin keeps trying to push glucose into your cells, but your cells no longer respond properly to it. At first your beta cells are able to produce enough extra insulin to compensate for your body's lack of sensitivity to it. However, as the years pass, your beta cells actually wear out from overuse, and their ability to sustain such high levels of insulin production gradually dwindles. When they can no longer keep up with your body's excessive demands for insulin, your blood sugar rises, which is when doctors make the diagnosis of diabetes.

While most people with insulin resistance continue to make enough insulin to keep them from developing diabetes, they often have other problems related to excessive insulin secretion, the most obvious and most frustrating of which is weight gain.

Here's how insulin resistance makes you fat: As you become insulin resistant, some parts of your body chemistry lose sensitivity to insulin while others remain sensitive. This creates an imbalance. The unnaturally large amounts of insulin that your body has to make to overcome insulin resistance in the parts of your system that lose sensitivity *end up overloading the parts that are still sensitive.*

One part of your body that stays particularly sensitive to insulin is your fat cells. Fat is where your body stores calories, and as previously noted, insulin is the body's main calorie-storing hormone. Insulin pushes calories—whether from fat, protein, or carbohydrates—into your fat cells.

Normally, between meals, fat flows out of your fat cells and into your bloodstream to provide energy and keep you from getting hungry. However, excessive amounts of insulin virtually lock fat into your fat cells, so your body can't use it for energy. This creates a frustrating paradox: You have plenty of calories stored up as fat, but you seem to be hungry all of the time. Your fat begins to act like a giant tumor, robbing you of nutrition as it grows. Scientists call this "internal starvation."

And fat indeed *does* tend to grow. Unfortunately, obesity actually makes insulin resistance worse, which creates a vicious cycle. Worse insulin resistance promotes more weight gain, which causes more insulin resistance.

Doctors have learned to recognize insulin resistance with a few remarkably simple tests. If you have any three of the signs on page 8, the odds are about 5 to 1 that you have insulin resistance.

- An abdominal girth measured at your navel of 38 inches or more if you are male, 34 inches or more if you are female (*Note:* Your pants size is not an accurate measure of your abdominal girth. You need to wrap a tape measure around your belly at the level of your navel.)

- A blood triglyceride level of 150 or greater

- An HDL ("good cholesterol") level less than 40 if you are male, less than 50 if you are female

- Blood pressure of 130/85 or higher

- Fasting blood sugar greater than 105

THE PROBLEM WITH Belly Fat

THE MOST common symptom of the obesity epidemic is the big belly. Television infomercials are devoted to wiping it out in our lifetime. Researchers are worried about the big-belly explosion for a different reason: It's the hard-to-miss symptom of insulin resistance.

Want a simple, informal (and official) test for insulin resistance? Grab a tape measure. Folks with insulin resistance typically have big bellies, even though their legs and hips may be quite slim. That's because, as the body's main calorie-storing hormone, insulin tends to pack calories into your abdominal fat, as opposed to the fat on your buttocks, arms, or legs.

Fat cells do more than store calories. They produce several hormones, some of which, in excess, can reduce insulin sensitivity and inflame blood vessels. Some scientists believe that because blood coming from the abdomen drains directly into the liver, excess abdominal fat is especially likely to aggravate insulin resistance and might even cause it.

Using a sophisticated scanning technique (positron-emission tomography, or PET), scientists can see where people store body fat after they eat different foods. It's unfair but a fact: While calories from fat and protein are stored all over the body, carbs go right to the belly.

If you have three or more of these signs, the odds are that your body needs more-than-normal amounts of insulin to handle the carbohydrates in your diet. Excessive insulin is locking calories in your fat stores so that the rest of your body can't use them to stave off hunger.

You don't need to starve yourself to lose weight; you don't even need to try to eat less. *You just need to reduce the amount of insulin your body makes.* There are two ways to do that: Reduce your intake of the carbs that are absorbed into your bloodstream too quickly—*the ones that cause after-meal blood sugar spikes.* Or *block the sugar* from those carbs. Let us count the ways that sugar blocking benefits your weight and health.

● SUGAR BLOCKING SQUELCHES AFTER-MEAL SPIKES

Your beta cells' job is to keep your blood sugar in as narrow a range as possible. Within minutes of your eating a carbohydrate, your blood sugar begins to rise. How high it rises after you eat depends on how many carbohydrates you eat, how much insulin your beta cells make, and how sensitive your body is to insulin.

However, that's not all: It also depends on how fast glucose enters your bloodstream. The reason is that it takes a lot more insulin to handle glucose that rushes into your bloodstream all at once than it does to handle the same amount of glucose that trickles in slowly.

If your diet is typical, most of the insulin you make is squandered on carbohydrates that are absorbed too quickly. In other words, it turns out that these after-meal blood sugar spikes are the main trigger of insulin excess. The key to reducing your body's demands for insulin is not necessarily to eliminate foods that break down to sugar but to get sugar to trickle into your bloodstream slowly instead of rushing in all at once. That's exactly what sugar blocking does.

People don't develop diabetes overnight. Their beta cells have trouble dealing with carbohydrates years before diagnosis. During this "prediabetic" phase, their blood sugar levels are okay when they haven't eaten for a few hours but often go up higher than normal after they consume carbohydrates.

To find out if you're having high after-meal blood sugar levels, check your blood sugar after you eat. You can do your own glucose tolerance test by measuring your blood sugar before and a couple hours after you eat a starchy snack. Normally, it shouldn't rise more than 40 points. If it does, you might have prediabetes, and you should talk to your doctor about it.

Indeed, that's why doctors do glucose tolerance tests to detect prediabetes. They measure your blood sugar after you consume a standard amount of glucose, looking for glucose spikes.

Blood sugar spikes are not just a sign of diabetes; they're also harmful to your arteries. Doctors now have monitoring devices they can attach to patients that record blood sugar levels continuously for days as patients go about their normal business. This allows doctors to tell how much the blood sugar fluctuates. Researchers have found that after-meal blood sugar spikes correlate better with blood vessel inflammation than do constantly high blood sugar levels.

● SUGAR BLOCKING CRUSHES CRAVINGS

It's no surprise that eliminating all carbohydrates reduces insulin demands and promotes weight loss. Your body hardly needs any insulin to handle other foods. However, if you've ever tried a strict low-carb diet, you know there's a problem with them: Even though you can eat all of the food you want, they're hard to stick with. Fruits and vegetables contain vitamins, minerals, and fiber, which are essential to good health. Eliminating them creates irresistible food cravings, which are Mother Nature's way of ensuring that you consume those vital nutrients.

You won't have this problem on the Sugar Blockers Diet. Several studies have shown that you can get the benefits of a low-carb diet without depriving yourself of foods that your body naturally craves. All you have to do is avoid a few carbohydrates—the ones that cause blood sugar spikes. For example, in a study reported in 2007 in the *Journal of the American Medical Association,* Boston researchers randomly assigned half of a group of overweight adults to a diet that allowed them to eat as much fat, protein, and fresh fruit and vegetables (all sugar-blocking foods) as they wanted but to reduce their intake of rapidly digested carbohydrates such as bread, potatoes, and rice. They assigned the other half to a low-fat, calorie-restricted diet.

After 18 months, the subjects who avoided rapidly digestible carbohydrates *without trying to reduce their intake of other foods* lost more weight than the participants who followed the low-fat diet, *who were trying to reduce their food intake.*

When you eliminate refined carbohydrates such as flour products, potatoes, and rice, you get the same benefits as cutting out *all* carbs but experience no cravings. Remember, Mother Nature never intended for humans to eat starchy foods like these. Starch contains no vital nutrients. (Any nutrients that grains and other starchy foods *do* contain can easily be obtained from other foods without the corresponding side effect of sugar shocks.) There is no biological reason to crave starch.

It would be great if you could eliminate starch completely, but the problem is that refined carbohydrates are sometimes hard to avoid. They've become staples of the modern diet. However, it turns out that you don't have to avoid them altogether. There *is* a way to make the glucose in refined carbohydrates trickle into your system slowly instead of rushing in all at once. And the results are astonishing.

VALERIE HAYES

Age: 58
Pounds lost: 18$\frac{1}{2}$
Inches lost: 9$\frac{1}{4}$

At 57, Valerie Hayes was pushing 250 pounds. Diabetes runs in her family, and her weight alone put her at risk. Valerie was motivated to try the Sugar Blockers Diet because she wanted to learn more about diabetes, which she knew was "quite sneaky."

With the Sugar Blockers Diet, Valerie got her health back on track and reached her weight loss goal. "It created a consistency in my day," she said of the program. "I had never been used to eating three meals. Eating three meals and planning out my day was a good thing—it made me more efficient. [Before the program] I would eat any time, [in the] middle of the night."

The food plan also helped her workout routine. Prior to the Sugar Blockers Diet, Valerie did exercise, just not consistently. Fortunately, the completion of the Delaware & Lehigh National Heritage Trail (conveniently located in front of Valerie's home) coincided with her decision to find out more about diabetes and stop the approach of the disease. She signed up for trail patrol and ordered Nordic walking poles. "I loved them," she said. Before she knew it, Valerie was using her walking poles almost every day.

Now the diet-and-exercise routine has become part of her everyday life, and a few weeks after the program's end, Valerie's weight loss was reaching 30 pounds—almost twice as much as her goal. Add in stabilized blood sugars and dramatic drops in cholesterol and triglyceride levels, and Valerie is well on her way to a healthier, diabetes-free life.

● SUGAR BLOCKING FEATURES FRESH, WHOLE FOODS

The fact is, fresh, whole foods like lean meat, nuts, fruits, and vegetables are full of natural sugar blockers, some of which block not only the sugar in food that contains them but also the sugar in other foods consumed with them. As you learned, your digestive tract has to break down the foods you eat to those basic building blocks—amino acids, fatty acids, and glucose—before they can be absorbed into your bloodstream. In a sense, the time it takes for this to happen is a natural regulator of the speed with which nutrients enter your system.

The problem, as you'll recall, is that our digestive tracts were designed for the Stone Age—made to handle food that was much harder to digest than the food we eat now. Our intestines evolved to be powerful extractors of glucose from unrefined vegetation, such as roots, bark, grasses, and unripe fruit and vegetables. Most carbohydrates in their natural form contain inhibitors to digestion—structures and substances that interfere with the breakdown and absorption of starch and sugar. It takes hours for the digestive tract to break down fresh vegetation to glucose and absorb it into your bloodstream.

But when carbohydrates are altered by humans—i.e., "refined"—they lose their natural sugar blockers. Indeed, compared with prehistoric times, many of the carbohydrates we eat now—particularly starchy staples like bread, potatoes, and rice—are ridiculously easy to digest. Whereas other foods require the entire 22 feet of the small intestine to be digested, starch and sugar get absorbed *in the first few inches.* This super-rapid absorption of refined carbohydrates creates a mismatch between the intestine's ability to absorb glucose and the body's capacity to handle it.

All sugar blockers do is restore, to some degree, a more natural balance between the kinds of carbohydrates we eat and the ability of our bodies to absorb them. A similar process occurs with other fresh, whole foods that contain lean protein (such as meat or eggs) and naturally healthy fats (such as fish or nuts). As you'll see, each type of food acts differently within the digestive tract to help slow the breakdown and absorption of glucose in the bloodstream.

Starch-Blocking PILLS

IN THE 1980s, with the obesity epidemic well under way, marketers of diet supplements came up with a product that they claimed prevented starch from being absorbed into the bloodstream. The powder, made from white kidney beans, contained a substance called phaseolamin.

Laboratory tests showed that phaseolamin could deactivate amylase, the intestinal enzyme responsible for breaking down starch to sugar. Supposedly, this white bean powder absorbed some of the calories in starch, so you could fill up on your favorite carbs and still lose weight.

Phaseolamin worked in the test tube. In the body? Not so much. It was discovered that stomach acid deactivates most of it before it reaches the small intestine, where amylase is. The government blocked companies from marketing phaseolamin as a weight loss product, and America soured on the whole idea of sugar blocking.

But scientists were intrigued. They knew that if you could deactivate amylase, you would indeed keep starch from being absorbed into the bloodstream. They got to work.

In 1999 the FDA approved acarbose, a proven-effective amylase inhibitor, for treating diabetes.

Acarbose works by mimicking starch. Like starch, it's made up of chains of sugar molecules linked end to end, but in a slightly different pattern from that of starch. The difference is just enough that when amylase tries to break the links between acarbose's sugar molecules as it does starch, it gets stuck and takes amylase out of action. Tests show that taking acarbose before you eat a starch-containing meal reduces your after-meal blood sugar level by about 30 percent on average and can lower it by as much as 40 percent.

From marketer's pipe dream to medical reality, acarbose works, both for preventing and treating diabetes and heart disease and for weight loss.

● SUGAR BLOCKING WORKS *WITH* YOUR BODY, NOT AGAINST IT

Let's say you're about to dig into a plate of pasta. You can sugar-block from the moment the first forkful touches your lips. That's because carbohydrates' journey from your lips to their final destinations—the cells of your body—is a long and winding path, chock-full of opportunities to head off a starch-induced sugar shock.

You might compare a carbohydrate's travels through your body to any widget produced at a factory. Raw materials are transformed into a finished product—in this case glucose, ready to be used for energy or stored as fat. To better understand how these body processes work, let's see what happens to that forkful of pasta.

First Stop

Chewing is the first stop of the journey. The smaller those spaghetti particles are when they reach your stomach, the faster you'll digest them. Thickness is a factor, too. For example, thin, wispy angel-hair pasta raises blood sugar more than large, thick lasagna noodles. If you slightly undercook your pasta (al dente) so that it's chunkier when you swallow it, it will take longer to digest, and raise your blood sugar less, than if you overcook it.

A Chance to Pause

Your stomach acts as a holding bin and a regulator of the speed with which food passes into your small intestine, where it is absorbed into your bloodstream. If it already contains food, your pasta will have to wait its turn before it can continue its journey. Carbs consumed on a full stomach raise your blood sugar less than those consumed on an empty stomach. Starting your pasta meal with a bulky, low–glycemic load food—say, a salad with lots of chunky raw veggies—will delay the absorption of those starchy carbs, reducing the likelihood of a pasta-induced sugar shock.

The "Speed Limit" Regulator

At the outlet of your stomach, a muscular ring, the pyloric valve, regulates the speed with which food leaves your stomach and enters your small intestine. Hormones and nerve circuits that originate in centers farther down your intestine control your pyloric valve—a feedback system that prevents food from passing too quickly through your system. When your intestine senses that more food is arriving than it can handle, it sends the message to your pyloric valve to tighten and slow the passage of food.

Your pyloric valve is all that stands between the pasta in your stomach and a surge of glucose in your bloodstream. When you eat fat, your intestine tells your pyloric valve to slow down. A few teaspoons of fat hitting your intestine activates a reflex that slows the passage of food through your pyloric valve. This will come in handy, as you'll see later.

Disassembly and Absorption

Once the pasta reaches your intestine, it has to be broken down into glucose before it can be absorbed into your bloodstream. Starch's long chains of glucose molecules must be split apart by the enzyme amylase before they can enter the bloodstream.

Once amylase does its work, the now-liberated glucose molecules in the pasta remain in solution in your digestive juices until they come in contact with the walls of your small intestine. Your intestinal lining contains "transporters" that latch onto nearby glucose molecules and pull them into your bloodstream. One way to slow the absorption of glucose is to eat foods that soak up intestinal juice and keep dissolved glucose from coming in contact with your intestinal lining.

Fruits and vegetables contain soluble fiber, which absorbs glucose molecules and prevents them from getting near those transporters. Soluble fiber is a natural way to keep glucose from rushing into your bloodstream. You'll learn more about it in Chapter 2.

The Filter

Once glucose gets into the blood that flows to your intestines, it has one more stop before it reaches the rest of your body. Your liver filters all of the blood that comes from your intestines. One of its jobs is to keep your blood sugar from shooting up too high after you eat. It removes glucose from your blood after you eat and adds glucose to your blood when you haven't eaten for a while.

Several natural substances—such as a properly timed shot of alcohol or a fatty snack—can help the liver take up glucose after you eat.

Sound the "Alarm"

Once out of your liver, blood from your digestive tract mixes with that coming from the rest of your body. Your heart then pumps it to all parts of your body, including the beta cells of your pancreas. These sense that your blood sugar is rising and respond by secreting insulin to lower it. How effective insulin is has a lot to do with timing. The sooner your beta cells secrete insulin into your bloodstream after you eat a carb, the less insulin you will need to lower your blood sugar. Your beta cells have a special supply of insulin ready to be released at the first sign of pasta heading toward your bloodstream. Just having food in your intestines even before more food enters your bloodstream, or simply tasting food, will cause your beta cells to release this cache of insulin into your bloodstream.

This is called the first-phase insulin response. Because this burst of insulin occurs so quickly, it keeps the blood sugar from rising as much as it otherwise would and reduces the total amount of insulin needed to handle a meal. There are several ways you can enhance the first-phase response. Protein triggers a first-phase response even though it contains no glucose. If you have a meatball with your spaghetti, it will increase the first-phase response and reduce your after-meal blood sugar surge.

Journey's End

Every cell in the body is surrounded by a membrane that regulates the flow of substances in and out. When a cell needs glucose, it sends glucose transporters to the membrane surface. These transporters pluck glucose molecules from the blood and bring them in to the cell.

Those transporters need insulin to be activated. But if a cell has all the glucose it needs, it stops producing transporters. Even if the blood that bathes the cell contains plenty of insulin, it won't take up glucose—it becomes "insulin resistant."

So the last part of your pasta's journey is to get across those membranes. Muscle cells are the biggest users of glucose and the target of most of the insulin the body makes. The reason you become insulin resistant is that your muscles stop making glucose transporters.

Exercise, on the other hand, makes your muscles switch on production of glucose transporters, which pull glucose out of your bloodstream and into cells. Those transporters stay on cell membranes for 24 hours or so, then start diminishing. As long as you exercise every 24 to 48 hours, your muscles will stay sensitive to insulin.

A Relief Valve

There's another way to get your muscles to remove glucose from your blood. Normally, when you exercise, it takes a few hours for your muscle cells to make glucose transporters and start responding to insulin. This presents a problem: If your muscle cells are going to use glucose as fuel, they will need it as soon as you start exercising, not in a few hours.

Your body has a way to solve this problem. Activating your muscles instantly opens up special channels in your muscle-cell membranes that

JIM AND TAMMY HOBAR

JIM	TAMMY
Age: 45	Age: 42
Pounds lost: 8$\frac{1}{2}$ pounds	Pounds lost: 8 pounds
Inches lost: 6	Inches lost: 9$\frac{1}{2}$

The Hobars found themselves simultaneously approaching middle age and type 2 diabetes. Tammy knew that she was at risk by being overweight, and her blood test results indicated that she was prediabetic. Jim, too, was struggling with weight and high blood pressure, and he has a strong familial history of diabetes.

In the past, both had shed pounds on other plans but found themselves hungry and suffering from headaches. However, with the Sugar Blockers Diet, Tammy said, "I'm not as hungry as frequently. I was more successful than on the other diets because I wasn't starving, I was able to feel full longer, and so I didn't quit." Both were even able to keep up the program during a family vacation to Hawaii.

Sugar blocking paid off, as you can see from their stats. But sugar blocking did more for this duo than help them shave poundage. "Overall, we eat much better," said Tammy. Jim, who does the shopping for the household, now pays more attention to his task. "I've started reading labels more," he said.

Best of all, both have brought their high blood pressure down significantly.

They also log more hours at the gym. Tammy noted, "I was at the highest weight I've ever been at. I was achy . . . and now I don't have that anymore. Instead, I have biceps!"

With blood pressure down, pain erased, and pounds and inches falling off, it looks like nothing but good things on the horizon for the Hobars!

are independent of insulin. Glucose flows into your muscle cells as soon as you start exercising and stops when you stop. One of the best ways to reduce an after-meal blood sugar spike is to get up and engage in a brisk 20-minute walk soon after eating.

So as you can see, you can block sugar at every turn from the minute you eat a carbohydrate. We'll dig into the many simple ways to do so next.

2

THE SUGAR
BLOCKERS DIET
PLAN

I N THIS CHAPTER, you'll learn the basic building blocks of the plan. First you'll learn which foods to limit. Second you'll learn what and how to eat—basically, how to fit sugar blockers and sugar-blocking techniques into your eating patterns. As you'll see, the program couldn't be simpler—or more effective.

● STEP 1: IDENTIFY THE CULPRITS

Most people squander most of the insulin their bodies produce on spikes in blood sugar that occur immediately after meals. So you don't have to avoid or limit all carbohydrates—just those that cause these "sugar shocks." How do we know which foods are the culprits?

Not All Carbs Are Created Equal

Not so long ago, doctors thought that, when it came to blood sugar, a carb was a carb. Whether you ate carbs in the form of veggies or cream pie, what mattered was how much glucose a carbohydrate eventually released into your bloodstream.

Or so they thought. In the 1980s, a group of researchers at the University of Toronto decided to test that assumption by systematically measuring the effects of various carbohydrates on blood glucose levels. They conducted hundreds of experiments in which they fed people identical amounts of available carbohydrate in different foods, then measured their blood sugar and insulin levels afterward.

What they learned surprised them. It turns out that not all carbs are equal. In fact, it's hard to predict from a food's carbohydrate content alone how much it will raise blood sugar. Most surprising was that some carbohydrates—white bread, for example—raise blood sugar as much as pure glucose does.

In the University of Toronto research, the blood sugar–raising effects of different foods were expressed as the percentage that the available carbohydrate in a food raises blood sugar compared with the same amount of carbohydrate consumed as pure glucose. For example, an apple was assigned a value of 39 because the carbohydrate in apple raises blood sugar 39 percent as much as the same amount of carbohydrate in pure glucose. The researchers named these measurements glycemic indexes.

Glycemic Load: A More Practical Measurement

The scientists who did this research weren't trying to create the latest weight loss bestseller. Nevertheless, several diet-book authors seized on the glycemic indexes as the hot new way for low-carb dieters to eat some carbohydrates and still lose weight.

But there was a problem with using the glycemic index as a guide to dieting. The amounts of food that the researchers gave subjects to measure effects on blood sugar *bore no relationship to the amounts people typically eat.* The glycemic indexes—while undoubtedly the result of solid, careful research—weren't meant to be used by real people in the real world.

Here's an example of the problems you get into when you try to use the glycemic index as a diet guide. Common sense tells us that a serving of pasta at your local Italian restaurant raises your blood sugar more than a carrot, but the glycemic index of carrots is 49 and that of spaghetti is 46. What's wrong with this picture?

Well, the Toronto researchers had a point to prove: that equal amounts of carbohydrate consumed in different foods can have different effects on blood sugar. To do that, they had to give subjects the same amounts of available carbohydrate in every food they tested. They chose 50 grams as the standard amount. The problem is that carrots contain a lot of indigestible fiber and water and not much *available* carbohydrate, which is the total amount of carbohydrate that a food contains *minus* its indigestible fiber. To feed their subjects 50 grams of available carbohydrate in carrots, the researchers had to make them eat seven full-size carrots. Who eats that many carrots at once?

Consequently, scientists at Harvard University developed a refinement of the glycemic index called the glycemic load, a user-friendly method of predicting the blood sugar–raising effects of various foods. The glycemic load, or GL, represents the amount that a *typical serving*—not necessarily 50 grams—of a food raises blood sugar. To be even more practical, researchers compared the results with those of a single 1-ounce slice of white bread. For example, a pear has a GL of 57, which means that eating a typical-size pear raises blood sugar 57 percent as much as a slice of white bread.

The reason the glycemic load works better than the glycemic index in real life is that, unlike the glycemic index, it reflects the blood sugar–raising effects of amounts of food that people really eat. A typical serving of carrot—one carrot—has a GL of 7. A typical restaurant-size serving of spaghetti—2 cups—has a GL of 276. Makes more sense, doesn't it? The GL more accurately reflects what foods do to your blood sugar in real life.

How to Calculate GL
THE SUGAR BLOCKERS DIET WAY

TO CONVERT the glycemic load values you see in other listings to those used throughout this book, simply multiply those values by 10. (In other words, in the International Table of Glycemic Index and Glycemic Load Values, the GL value for angel-food cake is 19; on the Sugar Blockers Diet list, it's 190.)

Why the change? We did it this way so that a slice of white bread would turn out to have a GL of 100. That way, the GLs of various foods can be regarded as percentages of that of a slice of white bread. For example, an apple has a GL of 78, which means it raises your blood sugar 78 percent as much as a slice of white bread does. We also adjusted for typical American serving sizes, which often vary from those in international listings.

The GL calculations produced valuable insights into the effects of various kinds of foods on health. Researchers found that diets that contain large amounts of high-GL foods raise the risk not only of diabetes and obesity but also of heart disease, menstrual disorders, age-related vision loss, acne, and some types of cancer.

Starches: Public Enemy #1

The GL measurements provide a framework for a way of eating that allows you to enjoy the largest-possible variety of carbohydrates with the least impact on your blood sugar and insulin demands. The table below is a list of the GLs of common foods that Americans eat, arranged in descending order so that the foods with highest GLs are at the top of the list and those with the lowest are at the bottom. Remember that the GL is the percentage that a typical serving of food raises blood sugar compared with a slice of white bread. In this list, instead of specifying *units* of food, such as one slice of bread or 1 cup of macaroni, we used amounts that people commonly eat. For example, people usually eat two slices of bread when they have a sandwich or 2 cups of pasta when it's the main dish.

Glycemic Loads of Common Foods in Descending Order

FOOD	DESCRIPTION	TYPICAL SERVING	GLYCEMIC LOAD (PERCENT OF 1 SLICE OF WHITE BREAD)
Pancake	5" diameter	2¹/₂ oz	346
Bagel	1 medium	3¹/₃ oz	340
Orange soda	12-oz can	12 oz	314
Macaroni	2 cups	10 oz	301
White rice	1 cup	6¹/₂ oz	283
Spaghetti	2 cups	10 oz	276
White bread	2 slices, ³/₈" thick	2³/₄ oz	260

(continued)

Glycemic Loads of Common Foods in Descending Order *(cont.)*

FOOD	DESCRIPTION	TYPICAL SERVING	GLYCEMIC LOAD (PERCENT OF 1 SLICE OF WHITE BREAD)
Baked potato	1 medium	5 oz	246
Whole wheat bread	2 slices, $^3/_8$" thick	$2^3/_4$ oz	234
Raisin bran	1 cup	2 oz	227
Brown rice	1 cup	$6^1/_2$ oz	222
French fries	Medium serving (McDonald's)	$5^1/_4$ oz	219
Coca-Cola	12-oz can	12 oz	218
Hamburger bun	Top and bottom, 5" diameter	$2^1/_2$ oz	213
English muffin	1 medium	2 oz	208
Doughnut	1 medium	2 oz	205
Cornflakes	1 cup	1 oz	199
Corn on the cob	1 ear	$5^1/_3$ oz	171
Blueberry muffin	$2^1/_2$" diameter	2 oz	169
Instant oatmeal (cooked)	1 cup	8 oz	154
Chocolate cake	1 slice (4" × 4" × 1")	3 oz	154
Grape-Nuts	1 cup	1 oz	142
Cheerios	1 cup	1 oz	142
Special K	1 cup	1oz	133
Cookie	1 medium	1 oz	114
White bread (laboratory standard)	1 slice (4" × $^1/_4$")	$1^1/_{16}$ oz	100
Tortilla (corn)	1 medium	$1^1/_4$ oz	85
Banana	1 medium	$3^1/_4$ oz	85
All-Bran	$^1/_2$ cup	1 oz	85
Tortilla (wheat)	1 medium	$1^3/_4$ oz	80
Apple	1 medium	$5^1/_2$ oz	78
Grapefruit juice (unsweetened)	6 oz	6 oz	75

FOOD	DESCRIPTION	TYPICAL SERVING	GLYCEMIC LOAD (PERCENT OF 1 SLICE OF WHITE BREAD)
Orange	1 medium	6 oz	71
Pinto beans	1/2 cup	3 oz	57
Pear	1 medium	6 oz	57
Pineapple	1 slice (3/4" × 3 1/2" wide)	3 oz	50
Peach	1 medium	4 oz	47
Grapes	1 cup (40 grapes)	2 1/2 oz	47
Kidney beans	1/2 cup	3 oz	40
Grapefruit	1 half	4 1/2 oz	32
Table sugar	1 round tsp	1/6 oz	28
Milk (whole)	8 oz	8 oz	27
Peas	1/4 cup	1 1/2 oz	16
Tomato	1 medium	5 oz	15
Strawberries	1 cup	5 1/2 oz	13
Carrot (raw)	1 medium (7 1/2" length)	3 oz	11
Peanuts	1/4 cup	1 1/4 oz	7
Spinach	1 cup	2 1/2 oz	0
Pork	Two 5-oz chops	10 oz	0
Margarine	Typical serving	1/4 oz	0
Lettuce	1 cup	2 1/2 oz	0
Fish	8-oz fillet	8 oz	0
Eggs	1 egg	1 1/2 oz	0
Cucumber	1 cup	6 oz	0
Chicken	1 breast	10 oz	0
Cheese	1 slice (2" × 2" × 1")	2 oz	0
Butter	1 tablespoon	1/4 oz	0
Broccoli	1/2 cup	1 1/2 oz	0
Beef	10-oz steak	10 oz	0

Did you notice that virtually every food with a GL of more than 100 (except for soft drinks) is a *starch*, while almost every fruit and vegetable has a GL of less than 100? Here's the bottom line: Fruits and veggies are carbohydrates, which your digestive tract eventually breaks down to glucose, but when it comes to raising your blood sugar, they don't hold a candle to starch. You'd have to eat seven peaches to match the blood sugar–raising effects of a bagel, or 10 cups of peanuts to equal the GL of a serving of spaghetti.

The reality is that for most of us, fruits and vegetables in their natural state don't raise blood sugar and insulin demands enough to worry about. They contain natural sugar-blocking structures and substances that slow the absorption of glucose into your bloodstream. The glycemic load measurements provide proof that the carbs you need to avoid are the ones that humans have *refined*—separated from their natural sugar-blocking constituents. The good news is that only a handful of carbs are responsible. If you're trying to avoid or manage diabetes or lose weight, don't stress about eating fresh fruit and vegetables—or eggs, meat, dairy products, or nuts, for that matter. *Just limit starches.*

Starches are easy to identify. Because of its physical properties and the way we customarily prepare it, starch is often blended into other foods. You can spot the culprits from across the room. The main offenders are bread and other baked goods (cookies, doughnuts, cake, etc.), potatoes, rice, pasta, and breakfast cereals.

Starch's Slippery Mimic

Sugar-containing beverages—soda, juices, and energy and coffee drinks—are the largest single source of added sugar in the American diet. A 12-ounce can of Coke, for example, contains 10 teaspoons of sugar. According to a statement from the American Heart Association, Americans consume just over 22 teaspoons of added sugar a day, most of it in beverages. Adults who consume one or more sugar-sweetened beverages per day double their risk of diabetes in 4 years, a study by Harvard researchers found.

The sugars in beverages go by so many different names, you might not recognize them. Besides plain cane sugar, common sugar sweeteners include high-fructose corn syrup, fructose, fruit-juice concentrates, honey, sucrose, and dextrose. If these ingredients are on the label, the beverage contains sugar.

Many people don't realize just how many calories their favorite beverages contain. While the calories might be listed right on the Nutrition Facts label, you need to make a distinction between a serving and the contents of the entire container. For example, the label on the 20-ounce bottle of your favorite drink might say that an 8-ounce serving contains 100 calories. However, the *bottle* contains 20 ounces—that's $2^1/_2$ servings. So while one "serving" of your drink is indeed 100 calories, you'll consume 250 calories if you drink the whole bottle—and most people do!

One reason sugar-sweetened beverages tend to make people fat is that they don't reduce your appetite. These sugary beverages contain mostly empty calories that don't satisfy the appetite. As a result, people consume more fluid calories in an attempt to get full.

People who drink sugar-containing beverages are often surprised at how easy it is to lose weight when they give them up. Our coauthor, Dr. Rob Thompson, told us that when his medical assistant, Nadine, who had been trying to lose weight for years, found out how much sugar was in the two Frappuccinos she was drinking every day, she switched to a different beverage. That change alone brought on 20 pounds of weight loss in 3 months, and she has kept it off for 2 years!

If you're the least bit concerned about your weight or your blood sugar, you know not to drink nondiet sodas. However, keep in mind that fruit juices—orange, apple, grapefruit, and cranberry juice—are also sugar-containing beverages even without added sugar. Think about it: All the sugar in fruit is in the juice. So when you take the juice from several pieces of fruit and put it all in one glass, you in effect create a sugar-sweetened beverage. You also leave behind the natural sugar blockers—the cellulose barriers, cell walls, and fiber.

Even if you include the whole fruit—for example, if you make a smoothie by pulverizing fruit in a blender—consuming fruit in liquid form increases its glycemic load. The reason is that you tend to consume more fruit when it's liquefied than you do when you eat it whole. In other words, the serving sizes are larger.

Sugar Can Be Your Friend

Dr. Thompson says that when he tells people that sugar is not their problem, many of them disagree, sometimes passionately. They *know* that the cakes, pies, brownies, and cookies they've been eating contributed to their expanding waistlines—and they're right, but not so much because of the sugar in them. What causes trouble is the *combination* of sugar and starch.

Starch is tasteless. Don't believe it? Eat a spoonful of flour. Pasty texture, no flavor. Yuck.

Now, take a spoonful of sugar. It's much too sweet—nauseatingly so. Also yuck. But mix the two in cookies, cakes, or pies, and it's a whole different ballgame. The sugar adds taste to the starch, and the starch dilutes the sugar, which tones down its sweetness. The result is that you end up consuming a lot more rapidly digestible carbohydrates than you ever would otherwise. As nice as it might taste, this butt-widening duo turns entirely to glucose in your gut.

So cookies, cakes, and doughnuts are out, but take heart. The glycemic loads of sweets that *do not contain starch* are not particularly high—much lower, in fact, than those of starches, such as bread, potatoes, and rice. The table below lists the GLs of some popular sweets. As you can see, the GLs of dark chocolate, peanut M&M's, and even pure table sugar aren't too bad.

POPULAR SWEETS	GLYCEMIC LOAD (PERCENT OF 1 SLICE OF WHITE BREAD)
Life Saver, 1 piece	20
Sugar, 1 rounded teaspoon	28
Peanut M&Ms, 1 snack-size bag	43
Dark chocolate, two 1" squares	44
Licorice, 1 twist	45
White chocolate, two 1" squares	49
Milk chocolate, two 1" squares	68
White bread, 1 slice	**100**
Doughnut, 1 medium-size	205
Cupcake, 2½" diameter	213
Brown rice, 1 cup	**222**
Baked potato, 1 potato	**246**

How can the GLs of candies be lower than those of bread, potatoes, and rice? It's not that they don't contain high concentrations of easily digestible sugar. It's because *the typical serving sizes are smaller*. Certainly, if you ate a pile of candy the size of a baked potato or a plateful of rice, you would raise your blood sugar as much as you would if you ate a baked potato or a plateful of rice. However, most of us don't need much candy to satisfy the urge for something sweet. A handful of it will do.

Because diabetics have problems with high blood levels of glucose—which, of course, is a type of sugar—doctors in the past thought that the worst thing a diabetic could do would be to consume sugar, the kind we use to sweeten things. However, the glycemic load measurements cast

Sugar BY ANY OTHER NAME . . .

SINCE THE 1970s, as Americans have been consuming less old-fashioned cane sugar and more high-fructose corn syrup (HFCS), our rates of obesity and diabetes have accelerated. Coincidence or no? Let's look at the facts.

High-fructose corn syrup is a thick, sweet liquid made from corn. During processing, some of the glucose in cornstarch is converted into fructose (which is also the main sugar in fruit). The sweetener contains glucose and fructose. Cane sugar—plain old table sugar—is sucrose, which also breaks down to glucose and fructose. The only difference: Cane sugar is 50 percent fructose, while HFCS is 55 percent fructose.

HFCS has contributed to our epidemic of obesity and diabetes, but not because it affects the body differently than ordinary sugar. A 2008 review published in the *American Journal of Clinical Nutrition* concluded that it was unlikely that HFCS caused the current obesity epidemic. Another recent report, conducted by the American Medical Association's Council on Science and Public Health, came to the same conclusion.

The problem with HFCS is that it's so cheap, we're now consuming a lot more of it. Using it slashes the cost of manufacturing all sorts of processed foods, including sweetened beverages. That's why we're offered those huge—and inexpensive—32-ounce Big Gulp beverages. In the 1950s and '60s, sodas were sold in 7-ounce bottles. Big Gulps would have been inconceivable back then.

---

sugar in a different light. The GL of a teaspoon of sugar is only 28 percent of that of a slice of white bread. If you want to put a teaspoon of sugar in your coffee or tea, or sprinkle it on some berries, it's not going to raise the GL much. Similarly, taking a few bites of candy after a meal has little effect on your blood sugar or your body's demand for insulin and can be quite satisfying.

So it's okay to keep some candy around to satisfy your sweet tooth. Just make sure it doesn't contain starch—no cookies, cakes, pie, or pastries. Candy tastes so good that it's easy to overeat, so be careful. Here are two rules of thumb for eating sweets: Eat them for dessert only, and don't eat more than you can hold in the cup of your hand.

All the Culprits You Need to Know

You don't need to try to reduce calories to lose weight. Just focus on eliminating two categories of foods: starches and sugar-sweetened beverages. That's it! In case you're unsure of who the culprits are, here's a comprehensive list.

Any kind of grain, including:

- Barley
- Buckwheat
- Millet
- Oats
- Quinoa
- Rice (white, brown, and wild)
- Rye
- Wheat

Foods that are made of grain:

- Bagels
- Bread (white, brown, or whole grain)
- Cakes, cookies, brownies, cupcakes
- Cereal, granola
- Chips, crackers, pretzels
- Doughnuts, muffins, croissants, pastries
- Oatmeal
- Pancakes, crepes, waffles

- Pasta, couscous
- Piecrust
- Pitas, tortillas, wraps
- Pizza crust

Potatoes and potato products:

- Potato chips
- Potato pancakes
- Red potatoes
- Sweet potatoes
- White potatoes

Corn and corn products:

- Cornbread, corn tortillas
- Corn chips
- Corn on the cob
- Grits

Sugar-sweetened beverages:

- Energy drinks
- Fruit juice
- Regular soda
- Slushies and smoothies

● STEP 2: LIMIT STARCHES WHEN YOU CAN

The Nurses' Health Study, a study of the diets of more than 120,000 American women that examined the relationship of glycemic load to obesity and diabetes, found that the risk of both conditions begins to increase when the average daily GL exceeds approximately 500. That's also the point below which natural weight loss occurs in overweight individuals with insulin resistance or type 2 diabetes.

WHY YOU DON'T HAVE TO WORRY ABOUT
Fat and Cholesterol

IN THE 1950s, researchers discovered that patients who had heart attacks often had high levels of cholesterol in their blood. Taking literally the old saw "You are what you eat," some scientists assumed, *without proof,* that high blood cholesterol came from eating too many cholesterol-containing foods. Similarly, it seemed to make sense that fatness probably came from eating fat-containing foods. Since animal products, like eggs, meat, and dairy products, are relatively high in both cholesterol and fat, the theory was that if you avoided these foods, perhaps you could lose weight as well as reduce blood cholesterol.

The problem was, the theory was wrong. Study after study has shown that low-carbohydrate, unrestricted-fat-and-cholesterol diets actually improve the balance between good and bad cholesterol, which reduces the risk of heart disease.

Make no mistake: High levels of cholesterol in your blood—or, more precisely, imbalances between good and bad cholesterol—*can* clog up your arteries and cause heart disease. However, high blood cholesterol decidedly *does not* come from eating cholesterol-containing foods; nor does avoiding dietary cholesterol prevent high blood cholesterol. What scientists then didn't realize is that your body makes most of its own cholesterol. If you eat less, it just makes more, and vice versa. Actually, the cholesterol in food is difficult to digest. Most of it passes right through your intestinal tract and out in your stool.

SANDI HAUSMAN

Age: 61
Pounds lost: 12
Inches lost: $5\frac{1}{2}$

Sandi Hausman started the Sugar Blockers Diet as a self-declared carb-and-Coca-Cola addict. In the past, it was easy to make excuses for a few guilty pleasures—especially as someone in good health who took daily vitamins. But once Sandi hit 60, she took a good look at her lifestyle—and realized that her weight was starting to hold her back. More and more aches were creeping up in her feet, knees, and hips each day, and her "numbers" (cholesterol, blood sugar, blood pressure), while they weren't warranting any medications, were high enough to alarm her.

Fast-forward a few weeks on the Sugar Blockers Diet, and Sandi is not even able to stomach the thought of a Coke. "In the past I could never give it up," said Sandi. But once she understood the negative effects that soda has on the body—specifically blood sugar—it was easy to give it up. And those aches and pains? Gone. Sandi's muscles are happy, and she's noticed that her old, nightly headaches are a thing of the past! And even after she finished the "official" Sugar Blockers Diet with a 12-pound weight loss in 6 weeks, she kept going: So far she's at a total of 26 pounds down and counting.

Sandi loves that the Sugar Blockers Diet, compared with other weight loss programs she's tried, is a natural fit with food planning. "There's nothing off-limits. We're going out with friends on Friday night, and we're looking forward to that. I just know what I need to do before I go."

How do you keep your daily GL below 500? You could add up the GLs of the different foods you eat as you go through the day. However, there's a much simpler way to make sure you keep your GL where it needs to be.

If you are typical, the GLs of the *nonstarchy* carbohydrates you eat in an average day—salads, vegetables, fruit, etc.—don't add up to more than 250.

It turns out that the GL of a typical serving of starch ranges around 250. So, to practically guarantee that your daily GL doesn't exceed 500, just follow this simple rule: *Don't eat more than the equivalent of one serving of starch a day*. You can eat a third of a serving three times a day, a half serving twice a day, or a full serving once a day. Just make sure the total is less than one serving of starch a day.

Simple. But it works.

A typical serving of starch fills about a quarter of a normal-size dinner plate. Here are some examples of a typical serving:

► 2 slices of bread

► 1 medium-size potato

► 1 ear of corn

TRANS FATS: No Starch, No Problem

IN THE 1960s, companies started promoting foods made with unsaturated fats, such as vegetable oil, as healthy alternatives to saturated fats, the kind in suet and lard. However, these products didn't keep as well as those made with saturated fats. Unsaturated fat becomes rancid after a few days at room temperature. To solve this problem, manufacturers developed a process called partial dehydrogenation, which extends the shelf life of foods made with unsaturated fat.

Scientists have recently discovered a problem with partially dehydrogenated fats. The dehydrogenation process produces an unnatural kind of fat called trans fat, which not only raises bad cholesterol but also lowers good cholesterol. Several cities have now banned products that contain excessive amounts of trans fat.

The good news is that if you avoid high-glycemic load foods, you don't have to worry about trans fat. Most of the partially dehydrogenated fats in our diet are consumed in refined and packaged starches. If you eliminate bread, rice, crackers, and chips, you get rid of the oils we add to make them palatable. You'll hardly have any trans fat in your diet at all.

- 1 cup pasta or rice
- 1 cup cereal
- 1 medium-size bagel or roll

Fake Your Favorite Starches

One serving of pasta, bread, or rice a day? Are you kidding? Don't panic. If you miss seeing starch on your plate, here are some substitutes for your favorite starches. Remember, starch is largely tasteless. When you replace it with the "starch impersonators or mimics" below, you will actually *add* flavor to your diet. In fact, you may enjoy your meals even more than before.

- **Swap pasta for squash.** They don't call it spaghetti squash for nothing! Cut a spaghetti squash in half and microwave at full power for 10 minutes or until a knife easily pierces the flesh. Using a fork, scrape out the squash into a large bowl and separate into strands. Voilà—you have a great substitute for spaghetti or any other kind of noodle you might want to enjoy. Zucchini strands can also work. Or try shirataki noodles, a Japanese noodle that is low in carbs. You can often find them in the refrigerated section of supermarkets or health food stores.

- **Substitute cauliflower for potato and rice.** It's white and filling, and you can bake, roast, boil, or mash it. Surprise! This versatile vegetable is cauliflower, and it turns out to make a very handy, nonstarchy substitute for potatoes. Try cauliflower in soups and stews, as a hearty side dish, even in "potato" salads; you'll be surprised at how similar it is. And the taste of cauliflower, like that of potatoes, is mild enough that you can season it any way you like. Cauliflower can also stand in for rice, believe it or not; just shred it into small pieces and microwave it in a couple of tablespoons of water for 5 to 6 minutes.

▶ **Trade in bread for tortillas or greens.** Instead of making a sandwich for lunch, for instance, chop up your sandwich fillings and serve them over salad greens. Not only will you get more fiber that way, but you won't be left with a huge head of lettuce rotting in your fridge because you've used only a few leaves to garnish your sandwich! Or, if you really want a handheld meal, wrap your fillings in a large piece of lettuce instead. You can also use low-carb tortilla wraps to substitute for bread. Look at the number of grams for total carbohydrate and fiber, and subtract the dietary fiber from the carbs. If the difference is 13 grams or less per serving, the wrap won't raise your blood sugar as much as a slice of white bread would.

THE **Must-Have-Pasta** SURVIVAL GUIDE

IF YOU absolutely have to have the occasional serving of pasta, it helps to follow a few simple guidelines.

Cook pasta so that it is firm, not soft. The common term for this is *al dente,* an Italian phrase meaning "to the bite" or "to the tooth." If you're not used to pasta cooked this way, it may seem undercooked, but it is in fact perfectly cooked. Most pasta packages give cooking times for al dente pasta; if not, simply cook for about 3 minutes less than the suggested time.

You can also cook rice, beans, and vegetables al dente. In general, the less you cook a food, the longer time it takes for you to digest it—and the slower your blood sugar will rise.

Opt for larger pasta varieties. Larger particles of food are harder for your digestive system to break down. So cooking your pasta in a way that creates larger particle sizes is a helpful sugar-blocking technique. If possible, when you choose pastas, favor larger varieties (such as lasagna) over smaller shapes (such as orzo).

Halve the starch, and go heavy on the (homemade) sauce. Add more sauces made with veggies, too. For example, a homemade pasta sauce, brimming with tomatoes, zucchini, onion, and eggplant, would give you lots of tummy-satisfying fiber and only half the starch. If you use only bottled sauce, opt for one made without sugar or other sweeteners, such as high-fructose corn syrup.

Baking the Sugar Blockers Diet Way

If you like home-baked breads, muffins, and cookies, you're in luck! You can add nuts, nut flour, or other nonstarch flours to any recipe that calls for regular flour in order to reduce its glycemic load.

The tips below can help you enjoy some of your favorite baked goods. Yes, they'll have a different flavor and texture. But aren't the benefits to your health and blood sugar worth a bit of experimentation?

Substitute half of any recipe's wheat flour with the same amount of nuts or nut flour. For example, if your recipe calls for 2 cups of regular flour, cut it back to 1 cup of whole grain flour, and substitute the other cup with 1 cup of nuts or 1 cup of the nut flours discussed below.

These simple swaps will cut in half the wheat flour content of cookies, muffins, or what-have-you. If you also add nuts, their starch-blocking effect will reduce the GL of the remaining wheat flour by an additional third. That means you reduce the GL of your baked treat by 66 percent!

One of our favorite nut flours is almond meal or flour, available in supermarkets or at natural-foods stores. Like most nut flours, almond meal contains more oil than wheat flour, so you won't need as much butter as usual. However, you will need more eggs to bind the dough, which is a bit more crumbly than flour because of the almond meal's lack of gluten. Whipped egg whites folded into the batter will also help lighten and raise the dough. Also, because the oil means that you have a larger amount of moisture in the dough, you will need longer baking times. For example, muffins made with flour usually bake for about 25 minutes, while muffins made with almond flour bake for about 45 minutes. Testing with a wooden pick to ensure that the center is dry will help determine doneness.

Nut flours are available from blanched nuts as well as unblanched ones. You will notice the difference in color: Blanched flours are more golden, while the unblanched have specks of skin in them. Using the blanched ones for baking creates a more typical-looking baked good, while either works well as a coating for meat and fish, as a topping on casseroles, and in other savory preparations.

If you're allergic to nuts or just want to experiment with some other flavors, try coconut flour. Like almond meal, coconut flour tends to be denser and to clump more than wheat flour. And it lacks wheat flour's gluten, which forms the structure of a recipe. Again, eggs will work to leaven cakes, muffins, cookies, and other baked goods. As a rule of thumb, using three eggs per $1/4$ cup of flour will create baked goods similar to standard ones. For fluffier cakes, try whipping the egg whites before folding them into the batter. Unlike almond meal, coconut flour can be a bit dry, so you may need to add more butter or oil and/or some pureed fruit (like applesauce) to add moisture.

● STEP 3: USE SUGAR BLOCKERS WHEN YOU CAN'T AVOID STARCHES

As you saw from Chapter 1, many foods contain natural sugar blockers, and your body has several ways of regulating how fast glucose enters your bloodstream. In the next few sections, you'll learn how to use sugar-blocking techniques to activate these natural processes, avoid after-meal blood sugar spikes, and reduce your body's demands for insulin. A warning, though: Sugar blockers only reduce after-meal blood sugar surges; they don't eliminate them completely. If you pig out on refined carbs, your levels can still shoot up too high. Sugar blocking doesn't give you license to eat all the starches you want. As discussed earlier, you should try to keep your daily glycemic load under 500.

As it turns out, the typical American dinner—when we take time to relax and enjoy one—provides an excellent framework for sugar blocking. Here's how it works.

LINDA FREY

Age: 52
Pounds lost: 17$^1/_2$
Inches lost: 13$^3/_4$

Linda had always resorted to sugary carb-laden snacks for comfort and quick hunger fixes, but her extra weight began to pile on when her mom got sick. Suddenly she found herself leaving work to go straight to the hospital to visit her dying mother without taking time to eat.

"I would get home around 8:30, eat carbs, then go to sleep. And I mean carbs—cereal, mac and cheese, pretzels, macaroni salad, tortilla chips." She knew she'd have to change her eating habits to get her body and health back on track.

On the plan, Linda traded in chips and pretzels for high-protein snacks like cheeses and nuts. The first 2 weeks felt like a detox as she learned to quell her hunger with raw veggies and her new favorite food: pecans. By the end of 2 weeks, she had shed almost 8 pounds.

"I feel more energetic, and I'm not huffing and puffing anymore," Linda reports. "My blood pressure has decreased, and I never thought my cholesterol would drop, but it did . . . even while eating eggs and bacon 4 days a week."

Linda was surprised at how easy it is to stay on the plan while dining out. Once she lets the waiters know at the start that she's on a low-starch program, they avoid placing bread on the table and are quick to recommend low-carb entrées and side dishes. Eating at parties is also surprisingly easy. "I found that hummus is a great party food to use as a dip with raw vegetables."

One thing is sure: Linda will be sticking to the Sugar Blockers Diet long after she reaches her ideal weight. "After those first 2 weeks, there was no looking back. I knew it worked."

- We often have an appetizer before a meal—the perfect opportunity for a fatty snack. As you've read, a small amount of fat consumed before a meal activates your pyloric valve and slows stomach emptying.

- We often eat a salad and a serving of vegetables with our meals. Both provide soluble fiber, the type that slows stomach emptying, soaks up glucose, and delays the absorption of glucose into the bloodstream. (More about soluble fiber later in this chapter.)

- We often use vinegar-based salad dressings. Vinegar partially deactivates amylase, the enzyme responsible for breaking down starch to sugar.

- We typically include a source of protein: meat, fish, or poultry. Protein consumed with starch triggers a first-phase insulin response, which improves insulin's efficiency so that you need less of it to keep your blood sugar down.

- Some of us enjoy a glass of wine with our meal. A modest amount of alcohol helps the liver remove sugar from the bloodstream after we eat.

- We save dessert for last. That way, if we slip up and have a little too much sugar for dessert, the sugar blockers in our meal help keep it from raising our blood sugar.

- Some of us go for a stroll after dinner. Walking removes sugar from the bloodstream without the need for insulin.

How about that? When you take the time to enjoy a traditional American dinner, you're eating in a way that makes it easy to use several sugar blockers. Moreover, they work on different parts of your digestive system, which is an especially effective sugar-blocking technique. For example, researchers found that combining a "sponge" type of sugar blocker, such as soluble fiber, with an enzyme inhibitor, such as vinegar, lowers after-meal blood sugar levels more than doubling the amount of either sugar blocker alone.

While it may not be realistic to incorporate every type of sugar blocker at every meal, a good rule of thumb would be to use three different sugar blockers if you are planning to have a serving of starch. In general, the more starch you eat, the more sugar blockers you should use. (And remember: *Never* eat starch on an empty stomach!) Let's look at these techniques more closely.

Eat a Fatty Snack Before Your Meal

Consuming a small amount of fat 10 to 30 minutes before you eat can lower after-meal blood sugar levels by as much as 38 percent. It does this by slowing stomach emptying. Your small intestine is highly sensitive to the presence of fat. As soon as a small amount of fat reaches your intestine, it triggers a reflex that shuts off the pyloric valve and slows digestion. It also stimulates a nerve pathway that helps your liver perform its shock-absorber function.

It takes remarkably little fat to have this effect. While you need a full serving or more of fruit or vegetables to inhibit starch absorption, as little as a teaspoon of fat—easily provided by a handful of nuts, a piece of cheese, a slice of bacon, or some oil in a salad dressing—will slow stomach emptying.

Although any kind of fat will block sugar spikes, be sure to include the healthy unsaturated kind. Two types of unsaturated fats that have particularly beneficial effects on the heart and blood vessels are monounsaturated fatty acids (MUFAs) and omega-3 fatty acids.

Nuts, avocados, and olives, along with olive, safflower, and canola oils, contain generous amounts of MUFAs. Happily, dark chocolate is also a good source of MUFAs.

Besides their sugar-blocking effects, MUFAs improve the balance between good and bad cholesterol. In one Pennsylvania State University study, high-MUFA diets lowered LDL cholesterol by 14 percent, triglyceride levels by 13 percent, and total cholesterol by 10 percent. MUFAs also lower blood pressure. Several research studies have linked olive oil consumption to reduced risk of heart disease.

Omega-3 fatty acids are found in the flesh of certain cold-water fish, including salmon, anchovies, mackerel, herring, and sardines. (Fish get omega-3s from feeding on algae.) Omega-3 fats improve your body's sensitivity to insulin, which reduces insulin demands. And there's also compelling evidence that they reduce blood triglyceride levels, stabilize the electrical activity of the heart, and counteract inflammation.

Go Nuts!

LOOKING FOR a fatty premeal snack? Go nuts! Whatever your favorite variety—almonds, peanuts, pistachios, walnuts—nuts are full of healthy fats, protein, and fiber and contain little starch or sugar.

Nuts have sugar-blocking powers. Eating a couple of handfuls as an appetizer before a starch-containing meal will reduce your after-meal blood sugar and insulin levels. Researchers at the Clinical Nutrition and Risk Factor Modification Center at St. Michael's Hospital in Toronto reported in the journal *Metabolism* that if you eat 60 grams of nuts (about two handfuls) with 50 grams of white bread (two slices), it will reduce the ensuing blood sugar surge by 37 percent more than eating the bread alone. If you have three handfuls, it will reduce the blood sugar rise by 55 percent. Peanuts and walnuts have the same effect; it's probably true of all nuts.

Beyond their sugar-blocking powers, nuts reduce blood levels of "bad" LDL cholesterol and raise "good" HDL cholesterol. Numerous studies have linked nut consumption to a reduced risk of heart and blood vessel disease.

Finally, nuts really satisfy your hunger. Test panelist Tammy Hobar noted, "Eating almonds while I cook dinner is twofold: It's a sugar blocker, but it also helps me eat less at dinner."

Start Your Meal with a Salad

It takes about 10 grams of fiber to reduce the after-meal blood sugar surge from a serving of starch by approximately 25 percent. No single, typical serving of fruit or vegetables comes close to providing 10 grams. You need several portions. Salads are especially helpful because they allow you to combine several sugar blockers. For example, a salad containing 2 cups of romaine lettuce (2 grams), a cup of chopped tomatoes (2 grams), and a cup of red bell peppers (3 grams) provides 7 grams of fiber. Add that, say, to a cup of broccoli (4.5 grams) with your meal and you have 11.5 grams of fiber. (For more "fiber-ful" fare, refer to the chart on page 57.)

Soluble fiber blocks sugar best when consumed before, rather than after, you eat starch. For example, if your meal includes a salad, steak, potatoes, and green beans, eat the salad and at least some of the green beans before eating the potatoes.

Use Vinegar–Based Dressing

Before insulin became available, physicians used vinegar to treat diabetes. For good reason: Vinegar is an effective starch blocker. Taking a couple of tablespoons before you eat starch reduces after-meal blood sugar levels by as much as 64 percent—comparable to the effects of prescription starch blockers.

You don't have to be a diabetic to benefit. Vinegar reduces blood sugar surges and tames insulin demands for people with insulin resistance but who don't have diabetes, which includes most overweight people and prediabetics.

Scientists attribute vinegar's starch-blocking powers to its high content of acetic acid, which deactivates amylase, the enzyme that breaks down starch to sugar. This explains why vinegar has no effect on the absorption of sugar, only starch. In other words, vinegar won't lower your blood sugar if you are going to eat candy, but it can help if you're going to eat bread.

In addition to inhibiting starch absorption, vinegar increases the body's sensitivity to insulin, which further reduces insulin demands and promotes weight loss. Studies show that vinegar taken with a meal lessens hunger for hours afterward. Go with your favorite variety—apple cider, red wine, or the more intense balsamic, which has a sweet-tart flavor. Whichever variety you choose, use at least 2 tablespoons on your salad.

Like salt, vinegar enhances food's flavor. Besides using it on salads, try a drizzle on meat or vegetables. Just remember to take vinegar *before* you eat starch, not after.

Eating pickles—which are full of vinegar and soluble fiber—is another tasty way to get vinegar. Research shows that consuming a full-size cucumber pickle before you eat starch significantly reduces your after-meal blood sugar level.

BALSAMIC VINEGAR: **Dark and Delicious**

BALSAMIC VINEGAR is a study in contrasts—sweet, spicy, sharp, or mellow. To create this vinegar, the juice of gently crushed wine grapes is first concentrated over an open flame. This sweet, thick grape mixture—called "must"—is fermented once by yeast to make alcohol, then fermented again. The process continues, often for years, as the mixture is aged in wooden barrels, resulting in the smooth, subtle flavor for which balsamic vinegars are known.

Unlike the sharp flavors usually associated with vinegar, balsamic vinegars are rich and dark, with a sweet-tart flavor.

While balsamic vinegar is perfect for salad vinaigrettes, you can also drizzle it on—if you can believe it—fresh fruit. For a unique treat, dip fresh strawberries in it. Delicious!

Add a Serving of Vegetables to Your Meal

Now we know: Mom was right to insist that we eat our veggies. The health and weight loss benefits of vegetables are numerous enough to fill multiple books and articles (and yes, at *Prevention,* we've written our fair share of them!). Vegetables are generally low in fat and calories and are chock-full of antioxidants, vitamins, minerals, and other nutrients. As if that weren't enough, they also turn out to be good sugar blockers. As we noted above, it's primarily the soluble fiber in vegetables that makes them such powerful sugar blockers. The chart on page 57 tells you which varieties of vegetables contain enough fiber to be considered sugar blockers—most of them, as it turns out. For the best sugar-blocking effects, cut veggies into the largest chunks possible, and don't overcook them.

In addition to their sugar-blocking effects, vegetables can often serve as delicious and satisfying starch substitutes. Said test panelist Jane Wilchak, "Roasted veggies and roasted cauliflowers—that became my new starch."

Include Protein with Your Meal

Researchers have found that a serving of protein can reduce by as much as 44 percent the blood sugar surge that occurs after you consume glucose. The amino acids in protein lower blood sugar by causing your beta cells to secrete insulin.

But wait—isn't the idea to *reduce* the amount of insulin your body has to make?

Although protein does cause your beta cells to secrete insulin, it makes them secrete it *sooner* after you eat carbohydrates than if you consumed carbohydrates alone—the first-phase insulin response. As you recall, the sooner your beta cells secrete insulin after you eat carbohydrates, the less of it you need to keep your blood sugar down. Protein consumed with carbohydrates causes insulin to act more efficiently, which ultimately reduces the amount of insulin needed.

Most of the protein in our diets comes from eggs, meat, and dairy products, although we get some from legumes such as beans and peas. Fish is not only a good source of lean protein but also an excellent source of omega-3 fatty acids, so we encourage you to eat more of it. Other than that, you can enjoy all your favorites—any kind of red meat or poultry is fine.

Consider a Glass of Wine with Your Meal

"I love that I can still have wine," said test panelist Wilchak. And if you're accustomed to pairing your meal with a glass of wine—or even a glass of beer or a cocktail—it can actually help keep your blood sugar and insulin levels down. As it turns out, alcohol has unique starch-blocking properties.

Here's how it works: Your liver normally converts some of the fat and protein in your blood to glucose, which adds to the glucose you eat. Alcohol consumed with a meal temporarily halts glucose production by your liver and reduces the contribution of that glucose to after-meal blood sugar elevations. Thus, a glass of beer or wine or a shot of hard liquor consumed before a meal will reduce the glycemic load of a typical serving of starch by approximately 25 percent.

It takes about an ounce and a half of alcohol—approximately the amount in a typical-size glass of wine or cocktail—to reduce your after-meal blood sugar. Translation: One drink is enough. Remember, calories consumed in liquids tend to add to rather than take the place of calories in solid foods. Consider, too, that alcohol delays the sensation of fullness from eating. Too much alcohol piles on calories and makes you tend to overeat.

Also, avoid cocktails made with juices (with the exception of tomato juice) and sugar-sweetened mixers such as ginger ale and tonic. Their GLs are too high.

Save the Best for Last

It's easier to pass up the potatoes and rice when you can look forward to something sweet for dessert. And on the Sugar Blockers Diet, you can have a little sugar. (Honestly, did you really think we would make you live without sweets?)

As you learned earlier, many sweets have reasonably low GLs. For example, a few bites of dark chocolate or a snack-size bag of peanut M&M's after a meal will soothe your sweet tooth with little effect on your blood sugar or your body's demand for insulin. Just make sure your dessert fits within your starch limit (the desserts in this cookbook are made with as little starch as possible and with sugar blockers like nuts built in as needed). Remember the two rules of thumb for eating sweets: Eat them for dessert only, and eat only the amount that fits in the cup of your hand.

SWEETENED YOGURTS
Are Not a Health Food

FULL-FAT, UNSWEETENED yogurts have glycemic loads as low as 10 percent of that of a slice of white bread and are excellent sources of protein. However, beware of most commercial fruit-flavored yogurts. Some claim to be low fat, but fat is not the problem. If you take a look at their ingredient lists, you'll see that most are heavily sweetened, with the result that they have GLs higher than 100 and should be avoided.

Try this instead: Use plain, full-fat, unsweetened yogurt, add fresh fruit, and sweeten to suit your taste. Put the sugar directly on the fruit. You'll probably find that you need only a ½ teaspoon or so of sugar, which has a GL of 14, to bring out the flavor of the fruit.

Similarly, low-fat ice creams often contain considerably more sugar than full-fat varieties. So go for regular or even premium full-fat ice cream. As long as you stick to a modest helping (¼ cup), the glycemic load is reasonable enough—30 to 40 percent of that of a slice of white bread.

Walk Off Your Meal

A walk sensitizes your muscles to insulin and helps lower blood sugar for 24 to 48 hours. However, there is another way that exercise can lower your blood sugar.

The contraction of muscles instantly opens up channels in your muscle cells, which allows them to take up glucose *independent of insulin*. Those channels open when your muscles start contracting and close when they stop. University of Wisconsin researchers found that a 20-minute walk immediately following a carbohydrate-containing meal cuts the after-meal blood sugar surge *in half*. So if you slip up and eat something you shouldn't, get up and go for a walk. Better yet, make it a habit.

Make Sure You Get the Sugar Blocking You Need

Because each type of sugar blocker works a little differently and works on different parts of your digestive tract, when and how much you eat of each sugar-blocking food is important. The chart opposite summarizes the amounts you need for effective sugar blocking and the optimal times to eat them. As you can see, you should try to consume most of your sugar blockers *before* you eat your starch.

● ABOUT NATURE'S MOST ABUNDANT SUGAR BLOCKER

All fruits and vegetables contain sugar; that's what makes them carbohydrates. However, they contain proportionately more fiber, so they don't raise blood sugar as much as starches do. Indeed, fiber is Mother Nature's most abundant sugar blocker, especially the type called soluble fiber.

There are two kinds of fiber, insoluble and soluble. Insoluble fiber is the stuff your grandmother called roughage. Made up of the tough husks and peels of fruits and veggies (which we typically don't eat), insoluble fiber passes through your digestive tract chemically unchanged.

Foods for Effective Sugar Blocking

SUGAR BLOCKER	AMOUNT	WHEN TO EAT
Cheese	½ oz or 1 Tbsp	10 to 30 minutes before starch
Fish oil capsules	Four 1,200-mg capsules	10 to 30 minutes before starch
Nuts	1 oz or 2 Tbsp	10 to 30 minutes before starch
Oil	1 oz or 2 Tbsp	10 to 30 minutes before starch
Vinegar	2 Tbsp	Before starch
Pickle	1 medium	Before starch
Soluble fiber	10 g (see page 57 for specific foods)	Before or with starch
Meat, fish, or poultry	4 oz raw (3 oz cooked)	Before or with starch
Eggs	2 whole	Before or with starch
Milk or yogurt (full-fat)	1 cup	Before or with starch
Chia seeds	2 Tbsp	Before or with starch
Flaxseeds	3 Tbsp	Before or with starch
Wine or beer	5 oz or 1 glass	Before or with starch
Liquor	1½ oz or 1 shot	Before or with starch
Cinnamon	2 tsp	With starch
Phase 2 (white bean extract) powder	2 tsp	Sprinkled on starch

Soluble fiber is abundant in the parts of fruits and vegetables that we *do* eat and is a more effective sugar blocker than the insoluble variety. Soluble fiber slows not only the absorption of glucose in the foods that contain it *but also the glucose released by other foods.*

As soluble fiber passes through your intestinal tract, it takes up fluid, swells, and gradually changes from solid to gel. As it swells, it soaks up fluid like a sponge, trapping starch and sugar in the niches between its molecules.

Soluble means dissolvable—and indeed, soluble fiber eventually dissolves, and the glucose it soaks up eventually gets washed out and absorbed into your bloodstream. However, that takes time. The glucose it soaks up seeps into your bloodstream slowly, so your body needs less insulin to handle it. Soluble fiber has been found to produce significant reductions in blood sugar and decreases insulin requirements in people with type 2 diabetes.

Soluble fiber also exerts what scientists call the second-meal effect—it reduces blood sugar not only after the meal with which it is consumed but also after the next meal of the day. Researchers at the University of Virginia gave subjects soluble fiber with their breakfast and measured blood sugar levels before and after both breakfast and lunch. The researchers compared the results with measurements in subjects receiving no added fiber. Soluble fiber not only lowered glucose after the breakfast meal but also reduced the glucose surge that occurred after lunch by 31 percent more than in the subjects who were not given added fiber.

Although there are plenty of good sources of soluble fiber—in addition to fruits and vegetables, beans, nuts, and seeds also contain plenty of soluble fiber—we still tend to eat much less than we should. The American Dietetic Association and American Heart Association both recommend that adults consume around 25 grams per day, but most Americans get less than 5 grams.

Fruits

The generous sugar content of some fruits counteracts some of their usefulness as sugar blockers. Although, thanks to the second-meal effect, they might reduce glucose levels after the *next* meal, the sugar they release nullifies the benefits for the *first* meal.

As fruit ripens, fiber barriers soften and the sugar content rises. Berries, peaches, and apricots have low GLs even when fully ripe. Pears should be eaten when still crisp. Tart-tasting apples, such as Golden Delicious, make good sugar blockers, but the sweeter varieties, such as Fuji and Honeycrisp, contain enough sugar to counteract their usefulness as sugar blockers. Dried fruits have higher GLs than fresh fruit simply because they're smaller, so you tend to eat more.

Vegetables

As a rule, vegetables block sugar better than fruits do; they have higher fiber contents and lower GLs. The rawer they are, the more effective they are. Boiling vegetables until they're limp and soggy saturates the soluble fiber in them, making it less effective as a sugar blocker. Also, the more crisp vegetables are when you eat them, the chunkier they are when they reach your stomach. Increasing the particle size of foods helps slow down digestion.

Carrots, broccoli, cauliflower, green beans, and asparagus all work best when they're cooked just enough to be able to puncture their surface with a fork. For example, Swedish researchers fed a group of subjects raw carrots with a starch-containing meal and compared their after-meal

GASSINESS: A Passing Phase

IF YOU'VE just added fruits and veggies to your diet, you may experience gassiness. That's because when their soluble fiber travels through your small intestine and arrives in your colon, friendly bacteria break it down into smaller compounds. While these bacteria help keep your colon healthy, the breakdown process produces gas.

To reduce gassiness, increase your fruit and veggie intake gradually. If you experience bloating, toot more, or develop diarrhea, don't worry—the discomfort will subside in a week or two. If you already eat lots of fresh fruits and vegetables, you may not experience it at all.

blood sugar levels with those of a group fed cooked carrots. Not only did the subjects who ate the raw carrots with their meal have lower after-meal blood sugar and insulin levels, but their "satiety ratings"—how satisfied they felt—were also significantly higher.

Beans

Beans and other legumes are packed with soluble fiber, but they also contain starch. A big serving can have a beneficial *second*-meal effect, but sometimes it can release enough glucose to give you a sugar shock immediately after the first meal.

Much depends on how you prepare beans. If you start with uncooked beans and serve them slightly crisp, ½ cup or so won't raise blood sugar much and can reduce the blood sugar–raising effects of other foods consumed during the first and second meals.

It doesn't take a lot of beans for you to get a good dose of fiber; just ½ cup of beans can provide as much as 8 grams. And as you can see from the table on pages 58–59, if you stick to a ½-cup serving, you're in no danger of raising your GL too high.

Don't cook beans until they're mushy or let them sit overnight and then reheat them. They become starchier and will often raise your blood sugar.

Nuts and Seeds

Nuts are not only rich sources of fiber; they also have other sugar-blocking qualities. They're tasty and satisfying and have negligible GLs. You can eat them freely.

Two good sources of fiber with proven sugar-blocking qualities are chia seeds and flaxseed.

Chia seeds. Imagine a balloon filling with water, and you'll have an idea of how chia seeds work in your digestive tract. They look like grains of sand, but each particle is actually a round capsule filled with compact soluble fiber. As the seeds travel through your digestive tract, they soak up fluid and expand to several times their original volume. The soluble fiber in them swells and soaks up glucose. University of Toronto researchers reported in the *Journal of the Federation of American Societies for Experimental Biology* that 1^1/$_2$ tablespoons of chia reduce the blood sugar–raising effect of eating two slices of white bread by 33 percent.

Chia seeds are also a good source of omega-3 fatty acids, which help lower blood sugar by improving insulin sensitivity. Further, in addition to being an excellent source of soluble fiber, they contain plenty of the insoluble kind, which is essential for good colon health. Chia imparts a slippery consistency to stools, which further aids bowel function.

Chia seeds have a pleasant flavor—like tiny nuts. They're considered a delicacy in Latin America. You can add them to practically anything. They go especially well with dishes you might put nuts in—salads, vegetable dishes, even ice cream. One tester, Cindy Swan, carried chia seeds with her in her purse so that she could sprinkle them on restaurant salads.

Flaxseeds. Flaxseeds contain high concentrations of soluble fiber, some insoluble fiber, and healthy omega-3s. Like chia seeds, flaxseeds soak up glucose in your digestive tract, which slows its absorption. University of Toronto researchers reported in the *British Journal of Nutrition* that adding 3 rounded tablespoons to a meal reduces after-meal blood sugar surges by 25 to 30 percent. Flaxseeds also raise blood levels of omega-3s, which increases your body's sensitivity to insulin. In addition, the fiber in flaxseed improves bowel function.

PLANT PARTS that are typically used as dietary supplements include psyllium, oat bran, guar, pectin, and powdered seaweed, all of which have been shown to reduce after-meal blood sugar levels. They're available in capsules or powder form at pharmacies or grocery stores.

Like the natural fiber in fruits and vegetables, soluble fiber supplements can reduce after-meal blood sugar and insulin demands. If you're already taking a fiber supplement—not a bad idea, considering that the typical American diet is markedly deficient in fiber—you can also put it to work as a sugar blocker. Although standard doses aren't enough to have much of an effect by themselves, they can enhance the sugar-blocking effects of the natural fiber in fruits and vegetables.

To help slow carbohydrate absorption, take fiber supplements shortly before you eat. For example, if your evening meal is when you are most likely to eat starch, take your fiber supplement shortly before or during your meal.

Flaxseeds have a pleasant, nutty flavor. You can add them to anything you would add nuts to, including salads or fruit and yogurt.

Fiber Up!

As we noted earlier, it takes 10 grams of fiber—about two large servings of high-fiber fruits or vegetables—to reduce your after-meal blood sugar surge by 25 percent. However, remember that the balance of fiber to sugar content is also important. The best foods to use for sugar blocking are those with a glycemic load less than 50, in addition to being high in fiber. Those with GLs between 50 and 100 are themselves acceptable to eat but release enough glucose to nullify their usefulness as sugar blockers. Foods with a GL higher than 100 may actually raise your blood sugar. Here's a handy list of low–glycemic load fiber sources, in order of fiber content.

Sources of Fiber with Low Glycemic Load

FOOD	SERVING SIZE	FIBER (GRAMS)	ESTIMATED GLYCEMIC LOAD
FRUITS			
Raspberries	1 cup	8.4	Less than 15
Blackberries (raw)	1 cup	7.6	Less than 15
Strawberries	1 cup	3.8	Less than 15
Avocado	½ avocado	3.5	20
Papaya, cubed	1 cup	2.5	30
Apricot	3 apricots	2.4	24
Grapefruit	½ grapefruit	1.4	32
VEGETABLES			
Artichokes (cooked)	1 cup	9.1	Less than 15
Sauerkraut	1 cup	5.9	Less than 15
Collard greens	1 cup	5.3	Less than 15
Carrot (cooked)	1 cup	5.1	Less than 15
Turnip greens (cooked)	1 cup	5	Less than 15
Broccoli	1 cup	4.5	Less than 15
Spinach (cooked)	1 cup	4.3	Less than 15
Brussels sprouts	1 cup	4.1	40
Okra (cooked)	1 cup	4	Less than 15
String beans	1 cup	4	Less than 15
Cabbage (cooked)	1 cup	3.5	Less than 15
Mushrooms (cooked)	1 cup	3.4	Less than 15
Cauliflower	1 cup	3.3	Less than 15
Turnips	1 cup	3.1	20
Dandelion greens	1 cup	3	Less than 15
Peppers (red)	1 cup	3	Less than 15
Asparagus	1 cup	2.9	Less than 15

(continued)

Sources of Fiber with Low Glycemic Load *(cont.)*

FOOD	SERVING SIZE	FIBER (GRAMS)	ESTIMATED GLYCEMIC LOAD
VEGETABLES *(continued)*			
Onions (cooked)	1 cup	2.9	Less than 15
Mustard greens (cooked)	1 cup	2.8	Less than 15
Peppers (green)	1 cup	2.7	Less than 15
Scallions	1 cup	2.6	Less than 15
Eggplant	1 cup	2.5	Less than 15
Carrot (raw)	7½" carrot	2.2	Less than 15
Lettuce, looseleaf	2 cups	2.2	Less than 15
Celery (diced)	1 cup	2	Less than 15
Lettuce, romaine	2 cups	2	Less than 15
Tomatoes (chopped)	1 cup	2	Less than 15
Bean sprouts	1 cup	1.9	Less than 15
Water chestnuts	½ cup	1.8	Less than 15
Cucumber pickle	1 large	1.6	Less than 15
Lettuce, iceberg	2 cups	1.6	Less than 15
Spinach (raw)	2 cups	1.6	Less than 15
Onions (raw)	½ cup	1.5	Less than 15
Lettuce, butterhead	2 cups	1.1	Less than 15
Alfalfa sprouts	1 cup	0.8	Less than 15
Cucumber (peeled)	1 cup	0.8	Less than 15
Mushrooms (raw)	1 cup	0.8	Less than 15
BEANS AND LEGUMES			
Lentils	½ cup	7.8	30
Soybeans	1 cup	7.6	Less than 15

FOOD	SERVING SIZE	FIBER (GRAMS)	ESTIMATED GLYCEMIC LOAD
BEANS AND LEGUMES (continued)			
Beans, pinto	½ cup	7.4	45
Beans, lima	½ cup	6.6	57
Beans, kidney	½ cup	6.5	40
Chickpeas	½ cup	6.2	45
Beans, navy	½ cup	5.8	40
Peas	½ cup	2.3	32
NUTS AND SEEDS			
Chia seeds	1 Tbsp	5.5	Less than 15
Almonds	24 nuts	3.2	Less than 15
Sunflower seeds	¼ cup	2.9	Less than 15
Hazelnuts	20 nuts	2.7	Less than 15
Peanuts	28 nuts	2.3	Less than 15
Walnuts	14 halves	1.9	Less than 15
Cashews	18 nuts	0.6	28
FIBER SUPPLEMENTS			
Psyllium husks	1 Tbsp	4.5	Less than 15
Oat bran (raw)	¼ cup	3.7	Less than 15
Guar gum	1 tsp	3	Less than 15
Metamucil	1 tsp	3	Less than 15

● DINING OUT, SUGAR BLOCKERS DIET STYLE

Whether you eat at a hamburger joint or chain restaurant or go in for ethnic cuisine, starch is on the menu at virtually every restaurant because it's filling and, above all, cheap. No worries. We've got you covered in almost any dining situation.

JOAN AND JEREMY GIANDOMENICO

JOAN	JEREMY
Age: 63	Age: 35
Pounds lost: 12 pounds	Pounds lost: 7½ pounds
Inches lost: 7	Inches lost: 6

Joan was growing frustrated with weight loss programs—she was putting in the time and not seeing the desired results. "I exercised 20 minutes, three or four times a week. I tried Weight Watchers and Jenny Craig," said Joan. But the weight wouldn't budge. Already struggling with high blood pressure and heavy weight—not to mention a family history of type 2 diabetes—Joan knew that she had to find another program.

She heard about the Sugar Blockers Diet through her son Jeremy, who was also participating. Five years prior, at age 30, Jeremy had been diagnosed as prediabetic. Because his father had type 2 diabetes and heart disease, Jeremy knew what that meant for his own health, and yet he hadn't been able to find a way to improve his risk factors. Even though he worked out 5 days a week, when he started the Sugar Blockers Diet, his cholesterol and triglyceride levels were so high that they were literally off the charts. "When I found out how bad my numbers were, I felt like a freight train hit me," said Jeremy. "I was devastated to see how bad [they] were."

As the weeks passed, Joan's postmeal blood sugar levels went down, and she also found herself feeling more satisfied after meals. "I wasn't hungry with this [program]," said Joan, adding, "I don't care for sweets too much anymore. If you put a piece of cake in front of me now, I think I would shy away from it." Joan also looks forward to exercise and enjoys the compliments she's getting from her co-workers about how good she looks. But perhaps the most gratifying results she's seen have been Jeremy's.

After just 6 weeks on the Sugar Blockers Diet, Jeremy found that his fasting blood sugar levels, which were 381 at the beginning of the program (high enough to be considered diabetic), came down a whopping 205 points, while his triglycerides improved by more than 500—by far the biggest drop in numbers across the board when it came to our test panelists. And he did it all with food! His doctor, Jeremy reported, was "very impressed with the test results I showed him," and his mother was relieved that he was finally motivated to make a change for his better health.

A Burger Joint

Most of the ingredients in a deluxe burger with all the trimmings—cheese, mayo, mustard, pickles—won't raise your blood sugar at all; in fact, some of them serve as sugar blockers. The problem is the bun. It has a glycemic load of 213—about the same as several slices of bread. Here are some tricks to help you enjoy a hamburger without spiking your blood sugar.

▶ Order a hamburger without the bun and eat it with a knife and fork. Cooks these days are getting used to serving burgers this way.

▶ Remove the top bun and eat it as an open-faced sandwich. You'll reduce the GL to approximately 70.

▶ Perhaps you don't want to fiddle with your burger—you just want to pick it up and eat it. It's *fast* food, right? Here's the hassle-free, ultrafast way to do it: Pick up the burger, and just before you take a bite, break off a bite-size hunk of the top bun exactly where you're about to take a bite, and put it in your starch pile.

▶ Instead of ordering fries, have a salad before your burger. Even McDonald's and Burger King serve them these days. The fiber in the salad will help reduce your after-meal blood sugar.

The Local Pizza Place

Most pizza toppings—the cheese, the meat—are low carb. The problem is the crust. The GL of the crust in one slice is 70 percent of that of a slice of white bread. Have three slices, and you're pushing your starch limit for the entire day.

Here's the trick. Cut away that big hunk of dough at the base of the triangle. If you do that, you reduce the GL by two-thirds. That means you can eat three slices without exceeding the GL of a slice of white bread.

A Chain Restaurant or Diner

Chains and diners have extensive menus—you should have no trouble crafting a low-GL meal. However, no matter how upscale a restaurant is, it will try to get you to fill up on starch so you won't want to eat so much of the expensive stuff. (That's why they bring you free bread before your meal!)

▶ Resist eating more than a half slice of bread before your meal. If you want a bite or two, break off a piece and slather it with a teaspoon of butter (or olive oil, if it's offered). Voilà—you've changed a sugar shocker to a sugar blocker.

▶ Most full-service restaurants offer a wide variety of hearty salads that contain meat, cheese, nuts, and vegetables. These are great meal options; the more of those ingredients a salad contains, the better it blocks sugar.

▶ If you opt for beef, poultry, or fish, forgo the customary starch that comes with it (fries, potatoes, rice) and request extra vegetables instead.

▶ Forgo dessert; restaurant portions are too large. Have a few bites of something sweet when you get home, or bring your own chocolate to the restaurant and sneak a few nibbles as you linger over coffee.

Mexican

Most Mexican dishes are served with rice or refried beans, which raise your blood sugar more than freshly cooked ones. If you skip them and employ sugar-blocking techniques, it's possible to enjoy a good meal without triggering a glucose shock.

▶ Chips, tacos, and tortillas made with corn flour raise blood sugar more than similar foods made with wheat flour. Avoid them.

- Guacamole is an excellent choice as a before-meal fatty snack. It contains healthy unsaturated oils and protein and won't raise blood sugar at all.

- Beware of tortilla chips. It takes only six measly chips to raise your blood sugar as much as a slice of white bread.

- Fajitas—strips of grilled meat served with sautéed peppers, onions, guacamole, sour cream, salsa, and tomato—are a good entrée option. However, fajitas are typically served with tortillas. If you must have one, ask for a wheat flour tortilla and limit yourself to one (the GL is approximately 85). Better yet, mix the ingredients together with your knife and fork and eat them without the tortilla. Delicious!

Italian

A typical entrée-size serving of spaghetti adds up to approximately 2 cups of pasta and has a GL of more than 400—way too high. Instead, do as the Italians do and limit your pasta to a *primi* (first-course) portion—1 cup or so—then take measures to soften the sugar shock.

- Italian restaurants serve great fatty appetizers (antipasti). Order one! They include caprese, which is sliced mozzarella cheese, tomatoes, and basil drenched in olive oil; carpaccio, thin slices of tenderloin dressed in oil and topped with capers and Parmesan cheese; prosciutto, thin slices of uncooked ham; and marinated olives.

- Saturate a small hunk of bread with olive oil and vinegar—both primo sugar blockers.

- Order a premeal salad with plenty of sugar-blocking ingredients and balsamic vinaigrette. Balsamic vinegar has a high content of acetic acid, the active sugar-blocking ingredient of vinegar.

- Have a glass of wine, another good sugar blocker.

- Order a pasta dish that contains plenty of other ingredients, such as meat, seafood, olives, olive oil, and vegetables. As you eat, separate some of the pasta from the other ingredients, and put it on your starch pile. If the dish is, say, half pasta and half other ingredients, and you push aside a third of the pasta, the sugar-blocking effects of the vegetables and protein should bring the glycemic load down to the point of giving you a mild blood sugar surge instead of a sugar shock. Then you can enjoy your *secondi* course—usually a meat or fish dish—without worrying about your blood sugar.

- Skip the tiramisu and cannoli and instead enjoy a cup of espresso, followed by a walk.

Chinese or Japanese

Chinese and Japanese restaurants have delightful meat, poultry, chicken, fish, and vegetable dishes that do not include starch. Avoid the accompanying rice, which, as you know, is solid starch. The glutinous rice used for sushi is especially bad.

On the Road

If you're traveling in your car, you can usually eat when you want and at whatever kind of restaurant you want. Air travel is another story. You're trapped in airplanes for hours at a time with nothing to eat but pretzels, or waiting in airports with limited selections of restaurants. You often arrive at your destination at odd hours and can't always choose where you will be when hunger hits. You're often compelled to eat things that you would normally try to avoid, such as starchy snacks or fast food.

One good trick is to bring along some nuts. They are good at quelling hunger and will put you back in control of your appetite when you're traveling.

If you plan to eat at restaurants during your trip and usually crave a bite or two of something sweet after meals, pack dark chocolate or some other starch-free sweet snack. Rather than eat the huge desserts that restaurants typically offer, you can have your own, more appropriate-size dessert later.

● HOW TO TELL IF THE PLAN IS WORKING FOR YOU

The Sugar Blockers Diet Plan is designed to help you lose weight and reduce insulin resistance by avoiding or blunting after-meal blood sugar shocks. Going to the doctor won't tell you how high your blood sugar rises after you eat a particular kind of food unless you rush in and have your blood sugar checked immediately after you eat it. But there are a couple of other ways that you can tell if the plan is working.

Using a Glucometer

If you have diabetes, you're probably used to measuring your own blood sugar with a glucometer—a portable blood sugar–measuring device. Even if you don't have diabetes, you can buy one at any pharmacy and easily teach yourself how to use it. Then you can see for yourself what various foods and combinations of foods and sugar blockers do to your blood sugar.

You don't have to check your blood sugar every time you eat. If you check it a few hours after you eat a particular combination of food and sugar blockers and it looks okay, then it's likely that your blood sugar level will be fine after you eat any similar combinations of food. (For example, if your blood sugar was fine after you ate a tuna fish wrap and an apple, it will probably be similar after you eat a chicken salad sandwich and an orange.) A reasonable goal is to keep your blood sugar from rising more than 40 points from where it was before you ate. If you have diabetes, you should try to keep your after-meal levels below 160. Levels of 160 to 200 are okay but not ideal; more than 200 is definitely too high. If you consistently get postmeal blood sugar levels higher than 200, examine your eating and activity patterns to see if you can pinpoint what's causing these highs.

When you reduce the glycemic load of the carbohydrates you eat and start using sugar blockers, you might notice a paradox: Sometimes your blood sugar level after you eat will be lower than it is the next morning. The reason is that instead of rushing into your bloodstream all at once, glucose is still trickling into your bloodstream the following morning. That's a sign that you are, indeed, slowing the absorption of glucose into your bloodstream.

The A1C Test

Every time your blood sugar rises, it puts a minuscule coat of sugar on the hemoglobin in your red blood cells, which stays there for up to 3 months. Doctors can measure the amount of sugar on your hemoglobin with a test called hemoglobin A1C. Your A1C level reflects your average blood sugar over the previous 3 months. If your blood sugar is always high, your A1C level will be high. However, if your fasting blood sugar is usually near normal but your A1C level is high, your blood sugar is probably spiking after many of your meals. Indeed, among people with prediabetes and those being treated for diabetes, after-meal blood sugar surges account for as much as 70 percent of abnormal blood sugar levels.

Normally, your A1C level should be less than 6. An A1C level greater than 6.5 usually means you have diabetes. If you have already been diagnosed with diabetes, your goal is to keep your A1C less than 7. If your A1C is between 7 and 8, most of the high blood sugar you're having is probably occurring after meals. The way to lower it further—indeed, the only way—is to get rid of after-meal spikes. With an effective sugar-blocking program, you can lower your A1C level in a month, although it will continue to decline for 3 months.

Mood and Energy

Sometimes you can tell what your blood sugar is doing by how you feel. When you eat something starchy or sugary, your blood sugar shoots up, which causes your beta cells to secrete a large burst of insulin. This sometimes causes your blood sugar to fall too fast. Most folks can't feel their blood sugar go up. However, they often feel it go down. Rapidly falling blood sugar causes weakness, shakiness, poor concentration, and dizziness. Doctors call this reactive hypoglycemia, or low blood sugar.

Blood sugar highs and lows can go on all day, causing alternating irritability and fatigue, which can leave you feeling exhausted at the end of the day. You can eliminate these symptoms by following the Sugar Blockers Diet Plan. "I don't even need to take my blood sugar to know it's going to go up," reported test panelist Michelle Newhard. "I tried a piece of cake at breakfast and was grumpy by lunch."

Weigh Yourself

Of course, the most obvious sign that the plan is working for you is that you are losing weight, For some people this will happen quickly—test panelist Scott Newhard dropped 8 pounds in just the first 2 weeks of the program—but don't be discouraged if your weight loss is slower and steadier. Your rate of weight loss depends on many factors, but rest assured that if you continue to follow the Sugar Blockers Diet Plan, over time you will shed the pounds!

BREAKFASTS

FRENCH TOAST WITH SOUR CREAM AND WALNUTS

Opting for sprouted-grain bread, which is naturally lower in carbs, and soaking it in a rich egg mixture blocks the carbs of the bread.

Prep time: 5 minutes
Total time: 10 minutes
Makes 2 servings

3   eggs
½   teaspoon ground cinnamon
2   slices sprouted whole grain bread
½   cup sour cream
2   tablespoons toasted walnuts, coarsely chopped

1. In a large bowl, whisk together the eggs and cinnamon until blended. Add the bread and soak until most of the liquid is absorbed, turning once.

2. Coat a nonstick griddle or large nonstick skillet with cooking spray and heat over medium heat. Cook the bread slices for 5 minutes, turning once, or until browned on both sides.

3. Divide the French toast between 2 plates. Top each serving with ¼ cup sour cream and 1 tablespoon walnuts.

Per serving: 331 calories ▸ 16 g protein ▸ 18 g carbohydrates ▸ 24 g fat ▸ 8.5 g saturated fat ▸ 4 g fiber ▸ 240 mg sodium

RICOTTA PANCAKES

These pancakes, stuffed with sugar-blocking fruit, eggs, and cheese, freeze beautifully. Let them cool, then place a sheet of waxed paper between each pancake. Wrap in foil or place in a resealable plastic food storage bag and freeze for up to 1 month.

Prep time: 15 minutes
Total time: 20 minutes
Makes 4 servings

3   navel oranges
1   cup raspberries
2   eggs
2   egg whites
1   container (15 ounces) part-skim ricotta cheese
1   packet stevia
½   cup whole wheat pastry flour
1   teaspoon baking powder

1. Grate 2 teaspoons of the peel from one of the oranges and set aside. Peel both oranges and cut crosswise into ¼"-thick slices. Transfer the slices to a large bowl. Add the raspberries and toss gently to combine.

2. In a large bowl, whisk together the whole eggs, egg whites, ricotta, stevia, and the reserved grated orange peel until well blended. Stir in the flour and baking powder just until blended.

3. Coat a large nonstick skillet with cooking spray and heat over medium heat. Drop the batter by 2 rounded tablespoons onto the skillet and cook for 3 minutes, or until the tops are covered with bubbles and the edges look cooked. Turn the pancakes and cook for 2 to 3 minutes on the second side. Transfer to a plate and keep warm. Repeat with the remaining batter.

4. Divide the pancakes among 4 plates and serve with the orange mixture.

Per serving: 317 calories ▶ 20 g protein ▶ 35 g carbohydrates ▶ 12 g fat ▶ 6 g saturated fat ▶ 6 g fiber ▶ 334 mg sodium

COCONUT WAFFLES WITH TWO-BERRY SYRUP

Here is a great use of coconut flour that turns a decadent meal into a sugar-blocker favorite! In addition to the coconut flour, the eggs, oil, and buttermilk also work to block the sugar.

Prep time: 15 minutes
Total time: 40 minutes
Makes 6 servings

Syrup
³/₄ cup blueberries
³/₄ cup raspberries
1 tablespoon Sucanat

Waffles
¹/₃ cup coconut flour
¹/₃ cup whole wheat pastry flour
¹/₃ cup unsweetened shredded coconut

1¹/₂ teaspoons baking powder
¹/₂ teaspoon baking soda
¹/₄ teaspoon ground cardamom
1¹/₂ cups buttermilk
4 eggs, separated
¹/₄ cup canola oil
2 tablespoons Sucanat
¹/₄ teaspoon salt

1. *To make the syrup:* In a medium microwaveable bowl, combine the blueberries, raspberries, and Sucanat. Microwave on medium power for 2 minutes, or until the mixture bubbles and thickens slightly. Let cool.

2. *To make the waffles:* In a medium bowl, whisk together the coconut flour, pastry flour, coconut, baking powder, baking soda, and cardamom. In a small bowl, whisk together the buttermilk, egg yolks, oil, and Sucanat. Stir the egg yolk mixture into the flour mixture until well combined.

3. In a medium bowl, with an electric mixer on medium-high speed, beat the egg whites and salt until stiff but not dry. Gently fold into the batter.

4. Preheat a waffle iron and lightly coat with cooking spray. Pour the batter into the waffle iron according to the manufacturer's directions. Close and cook for 3 to 5 minutes, or until the steaming stops and the waffles are crisp. Repeat to make 6 waffles. Serve with the syrup.

Per serving: 278 calories ► 8 g protein ► 24 g carbohydrates ► 17 g fat ► 5 g saturated fat ► 6 g fiber ► 440 mg sodium

ORANGE-RASPBERRY CLAFOUTI

This refreshing breakfast is a great alternative to the more traditional favorites like omelets and scrambled eggs. Bursting with sugar blockers—eggs, milk, butter, and walnuts—it makes a breakfast lovely enough for company.

Prep time: 10 minutes
Total time: 1 hour
Makes 6 servings

2   cups fresh or frozen raspberries
½   cup walnuts, finely chopped
¾   cup milk
4   eggs
½   cup whole wheat pastry flour
3   tablespoons Sucanat
2   tablespoons butter, melted
1   tablespoon grated orange peel
1   teaspoon vanilla extract
      Pinch of salt

1. Preheat the oven to 350°F. Coat a 9" pie plate with cooking spray. Spoon the raspberries into the pie plate. Scatter the walnuts over the raspberries.

2. In a food processor or blender, combine the milk, eggs, flour, Sucanat, butter, orange peel, vanilla, and salt and process until smooth. Pour the batter over the raspberry mixture.

3. Bake for 40 minutes, or until the top is golden and a knife inserted in the center comes out clean. Let cool for 15 minutes to serve warm, or serve at room temperature.

Per serving: 241 calories ▸ 8 g protein ▸ 20 g carbohydrates ▸ 15 g fat ▸ 4.5 g saturated fat ▸ 4 g fiber ▸ 113 mg sodium

BRAN MUFFINS

The muffins can be stored in an airtight container up to 2 days at room temperature or in the freezer for up to 2 months.

Prep time: 40 minutes
Total time: 1 hour
Makes 12

1 cup shredded bran cereal with extra fiber
3 tablespoons olive oil
½ cup boiling water
1 cup buttermilk
1 egg
2 tablespoons molasses
½ cup whole wheat pastry flour
¼ cup almond flour
¼ cup oat bran
1 teaspoon baking soda
¼ teaspoon salt
⅓ cup walnuts, chopped

1. Preheat the oven to 375°F. Line a 12-cup muffin pan with paper liners or coat with cooking spray.

2. In a large heatproof bowl, combine the cereal and oil. Add the boiling water and stir to combine. Let cool for 15 minutes.

3. In a measuring cup, beat the buttermilk, egg, and molasses until blended. Add to the cereal mixture and stir until combined.

4. In a small bowl, whisk together the whole wheat flour, almond flour, oat bran, baking soda, and salt. Stir the flour mixture and walnuts into the cereal mixture. Stir just until moistened. Cover the bowl and let stand for 15 minutes.

5. Divide the batter among the muffin cups. Bake for 20 minutes, or until a wooden pick inserted in the center of a muffin comes out clean. Let cool for 5 minutes in the pan on a rack before removing.

Per muffin: 120 calories ▶ 4 g protein ▶ 12 g carbohydrates ▶ 8 g fat ▶ 1 g saturated fat ▶ 3 g fiber ▶ 196 mg sodium

LOX BREAKFAST SANDWICH

Here's our version of lox and bagels without the carb overload. For a variation or a snack, spread the tortilla with 1 tablespoon cream cheese, top with the lox, a few slices of thinly sliced red onion, cucumber, and a sprinkling of lemon juice.

Prep time: 10 minutes
Total time: 10 minutes
Makes 2 servings

1 cup chopped mixed baby greens
1 tablespoon fresh lemon juice
1 teaspoon olive oil
⅛ teaspoon ground black pepper
2 low-carb tortillas (7" diameter)
4 ounces smoked salmon
½ Hass avocado, pitted, peeled, and thinly sliced

1. In a large bowl, combine the greens, lemon juice, oil, and pepper, tossing until well mixed.

2. Place 1 tortilla on a flat surface. Layer half of the greens, smoked salmon, and avocado down the center. Fold the short sides over the filling, then roll up burrito style to enclose the filling. Repeat to make 1 more wrap. Cut each wrap in half and serve at once.

Per serving: 363 calories ▶ 41 g protein ▶ 18 g carbohydrates ▶ 18 g fat ▶ 3 g saturated fat ▶ 13 g fiber ▶ 51 mg sodium

ICED FRUIT SHAKE

Whip up this shake in minutes for a fast yet flavorful breakfast smoothie. Be sure to use protein powder that is low carb—some are loaded with sugar—for a sugar-blocking start to the day.

Prep time: 5 minutes
Total time: 5 minutes
Makes 4 servings

1   cup frozen peaches
1   cup frozen unsweetened strawberries
2   cups whole milk
1   cup vanilla protein powder
½   cup ice cubes

In a blender, combine the peaches, strawberries, milk, protein powder, and ice cubes. Process for 2 minutes, or until smooth.

Per serving: 230 calories ▶ 13 g protein ▶ 27 g carbohydrates ▶ 8 g fat ▶ 2 g saturated fat ▶ 9 g fiber ▶ 53 mg sodium

NUTTY GRANOLA

For a delicious but fast breakfast, serve ¼ cup of the granola with ½ cup each plain Greek yogurt and raspberries.

Prep time: 10 minutes
Total time: 45 minutes
Makes 6 cups

- 3 cups old-fashioned rolled oats
- 1 cup sliced almonds
- 1 cup unsalted dry-roasted peanuts
- ¼ cup shelled pumpkin seeds
- ¼ cup flaxseeds
- ¼ cup canola oil
- ¼ cup Sucanat
- 1 tablespoon ground cinnamon
- 1 tablespoon ground nutmeg
- 1 tablespoon almond extract

1. Preheat the oven to 300°F. Coat a rimmed baking sheet with cooking spray. Combine the oats, almonds, peanuts, pumpkin seeds, and flaxseeds in the pan.

2. In a small saucepan, heat the oil, Sucanat, cinnamon, and nutmeg over medium-low heat. Cook for 3 minutes, stirring, or until the Sucanat is completely dissolved. Remove from the heat. Stir in the almond extract. Drizzle over the oat mixture, stirring with a wooden spoon until evenly coated. Spread the oat mixture out on the pan.

3. Bake for 30 minutes, stirring occasionally, or until golden brown. Let cool completely.

....

Per ¼-cup serving: 147 calories ► 5 g protein ► 10 g carbohydrates ► 10 g fat ► 1 g saturated fat ► 3 g fiber ► 3 mg sodium

TROPICAL MELON IN COTTAGE CHEESE

To toast coconut, place in a small dry skillet over low heat and cook for 1 to 2 minutes, stirring and shaking the pan often, or until lightly browned.

Prep time: 10 minutes
Total time: 10 minutes
Makes 4 servings

- 2   cups small curd cottage cheese
- 1   cup cubed cantaloupe
- 1   cup cubed honeydew melon
- ¼   cup toasted chopped macadamia nuts
- 4   teaspoons unsweetened shredded coconut, toasted

Divide the cottage cheese among 4 bowls and top with the cantaloupe, honeydew, nuts, and coconut.

Per serving: 192 calories ► 15 g protein ► 13 g carbohydrates ► 10 g fat ► 2.5 g saturated fat ► 2 g fiber ► 388 mg sodium

TOMATO, BASIL, AND GOAT CHEESE SCRAMBLE

The fresh Mediterranean flavors of this dish make it ideal for a brunch or a light summer meal.

Prep time: 10 minutes
Total time: 15 minutes
Makes 2 servings

6 eggs
¼ teaspoon salt
¼ teaspoon ground black pepper
⅓ cup chopped sun-dried tomatoes
¼ cup fresh basil leaves, torn
2 ounces goat cheese, crumbled

1. In a large bowl, beat the eggs, salt, and pepper until well blended. Add the sun-dried tomatoes and basil and stir until well combined.

2. Coat a large nonstick skillet with cooking spray and heat over medium heat. Cook the egg mixture for 3 to 4 minutes, stirring occasionally, or until the eggs are softly scrambled but still moist and creamy. Sprinkle with the cheese and cook for 1 minute, or until the cheese melts.

Per serving: 358 calories ▶ 26 g protein ▶ 6 g carbohydrates ▶ 26 g fat ▶ 11 g saturated fat ▶ 1 g fiber ▶ 70 mg sodium

MEDITERRANEAN FRITTATA

Refrigerated potatoes are already cut and pre-cooked, saving a lot of prep work. You can find them in the meat or dairy section of your supermarket.

Prep time: 10 minutes
Total time: 35 minutes
Makes 6 servings

2 tablespoons olive oil
1 cup refrigerated diced potatoes
¼ cup sliced mushrooms
1 tomato, chopped
¼ cup pitted sliced kalamata olives
6 eggs
¼ cup water
½ teaspoon ground black pepper
½ cup crumbled goat cheese

1. Warm the oil in a large nonstick skillet over medium-high heat. Spread the potatoes evenly over the bottom of the pan and cook for 6 minutes, stirring occasionally, or until the potatoes brown and begin to crisp. Add the mushrooms and cook for 5 minutes, or until the mushrooms are softened. Stir in the tomato and olives and cook for 1 minute, stirring, or until softened.

2. Meanwhile, in a large bowl, beat the eggs, water, and pepper until well blended.

3. Pour the egg mixture into the skillet and cook for 7 minutes, gently lifting the edges to let the uncooked portion flow underneath, or until the eggs are partially set.

4. Sprinkle the cheese evenly over the frittata, cover, and cook for 1 to 2 minutes, or until the cheese is just melted and the frittata is completely set. Cut into wedges to serve.

Per serving: 183 calories ▶ 9 g protein ▶ 6 g carbohydrates ▶ 14 g fat ▶ 4.5 g saturated fat ▶ 1 g fiber ▶ 266 mg sodium

ITALIAN OMELET

Whether you're cooking omelets for 2 or 20, choose easy fillings that require no cooking. Here drained strips of roasted red peppers from a jar fit the bill. Other easy fillings are store-bought pesto or tapenade with diced tomatoes, diced ham and Brie cheese, or goat cheese with chopped fresh herbs.

Prep time: 10 minutes
Total time: 25 minutes
Makes 4 servings

8   eggs
¾   cup whole milk
½   teaspoon salt
¼   teaspoon ground black pepper
1   cup roasted red pepper strips, drained and patted dry
1   teaspoon dried oregano
1   clove garlic, minced
4   teaspoons butter, at room temperature, divided
1   cup shredded part-skim mozzarella cheese

1. In a large bowl, whisk together the eggs, milk, salt, and black pepper. In a small bowl, combine the red pepper strips, oregano, and garlic.

2. Heat 1 teaspoon of the butter in a medium nonstick skillet over medium heat. Pour about ⅔ cup of the egg mixture into the skillet. Cook for 3 minutes, lifting the edges frequently with a spatula to allow the uncooked egg to run underneath, or until the eggs are just set. Spoon ¼ cup of the roasted pepper mixture on one half of the omelet. Top with ¼ cup of the mozzarella. Fold over the other half of the omelet to cover the filling.

3. Slide the omelet onto a plate. Keep warm. Repeat with the remaining egg mixture and roasted pepper mixture to make 3 more omelets.

Per serving: 339 calories ▸ 23 g protein ▸ 12 g carbohydrates ▸ 22 g fat ▸ 9.5 g saturated fat ▸ 3 g fiber ▸ 775 mg sodium

ZUCCHINI BAKED EGGS

These eggs are perfect for brunch. Simply prepare them ahead of time and pop into the oven just before serving.

Prep time: 10 minutes
Total time: 35 minutes
Makes 4 servings

- 2   teaspoons olive oil
- 2   teaspoons butter
- 1   zucchini, thinly sliced
- ½   small onion, chopped
- ½   teaspoon dried basil
- ½   teaspoon salt
- ¼   teaspoon ground black pepper
- 8   eggs
- 4   teaspoons heavy cream
- ¼   cup shredded Swiss or provolone cheese

1. Preheat the oven to 350°F. Spray four 6-ounce custard cups with cooking spray.

2. In a large nonstick skillet over medium-high heat, heat the oil and butter. Cook the zucchini, onion, basil, salt, and pepper for 8 minutes, stirring occasionally, or until the vegetables are tender.

3. Divide the zucchini mixture among the custard cups. Carefully break 2 eggs into each custard cup. Top each egg with 1 teaspoon cream and sprinkle with 1 tablespoon cheese.

4. Place the custard cups on a small rimmed baking sheet. Cover with foil and bake for 10 minutes, or until the whites are opaque and the yolks are set.

Per serving: 242 calories ▶ 16 g protein ▶ 6 g carbohydrates ▶ 18 g fat ▶ 7 g saturated fat ▶ 2 g fiber ▶ 519 mg sodium

TEX-MEX EGGS

Add ½ cup finely chopped red bell pepper to the egg mixture before cooking.

Prep time: 5 minutes
Total time: 15 minutes
Makes 4 servings

4   low-carb tortillas (7" diameter)
6   eggs
⅛   teaspoon ground black pepper
4   ounces low-sodium ham, finely chopped
1½ teaspoons butter
1   cup salsa
1   cup shredded Cheddar cheese

1. Wrap the tortillas in paper towels and microwave on medium power for 30 seconds, or until warm.

2. Meanwhile, in a large bowl, whisk the eggs and pepper until blended. Stir in the ham.

3. Heat the butter in a large nonstick skillet over medium heat. Add the egg mixture and reduce the heat to medium-low. Cook for 2 minutes, stirring, or until the eggs are softly scrambled but still moist and creamy.

4. Divide the tortillas among 4 plates. Spoon one-fourth of the egg mixture onto the bottom half of each tortilla. Top each one with ¼ cup salsa and ¼ cup cheese. Fold the sides in, and roll up from the bottom, burrito style. Cut in half with a serrated knife.

Per serving: 320 calories ► 24 g protein ► 14 g carbohydrates ► 22 g fat ► 10 g saturated fat ► 8 g fiber ► 692 mg sodium

TARRAGON-RICOTTA SOUFFLÉS

Perfect for brunch or dinner, these savory soufflés—accented with orange peel and delicate tarragon—are a little more forgiving than traditional soufflés because the ricotta adds a fair amount of stability.

Prep time: 20 minutes
Total time: 45 minutes
Makes 4 servings

1   tablespoon butter
2   tablespoons all-purpose flour
1   cup low-fat evaporated milk
⅓   cup part-skim ricotta cheese
¼   cup grated Parmesan cheese
4   eggs, separated
1   tablespoon finely chopped fresh tarragon
1½ teaspoons grated orange peel
½   teaspoon salt
⅛   teaspoon ground black pepper
½   teaspoon cream of tartar

1. Preheat the oven to 400°F. Coat four 8-ounce ramekins, soufflé dishes, or custard cups with cooking spray.

2. Melt the butter in a small saucepan over medium heat. Add the flour and cook, stirring, for 1 minute. Whisk in the evaporated milk and bring to a boil, whisking constantly until the mixture begins to thicken. Remove from the heat.

3. In a large bowl, combine the ricotta, Parmesan, egg yolks, tarragon, orange peel, salt, and pepper until well mixed. Gradually whisk in the hot milk mixture until blended and smooth.

4. In a medium bowl, with an electric mixer on medium speed, beat the egg whites and cream of tartar for 3 minutes, or until stiff, glossy peaks form. With a rubber spatula, stir about one-quarter of the beaten egg whites into the ricotta mixture to lighten it. Then gently fold in the remaining egg whites until no white streaks remain.

5. Spoon the batter into the ramekins, filling each about three-quarters full. Place the dishes in a roasting pan lined with a kitchen towel to prevent them from slipping. Place the pan in the oven, then carefully fill the roasting pan with hot water until it reaches two-thirds up the sides of the soufflé dishes. Bake for 25 minutes, or until golden brown and puffed.

Per serving: 240 calories ► 17 g protein ► 12 g carbohydrates ► 14 g fat ► 7 g saturated fat ► 0 g fiber ► 530 mg sodium

HAM AND SWISS QUESADILLA

Add half of a Granny Smith apple, cut into thin slices, to the filling if you like.

Prep time: 5 minutes
Total time: 10 minutes
Makes 1 serving

---

1   low-carb tortilla (7" diameter)
1   ounce deli-sliced ham
½   red bell pepper, cut into thin strips
¼   cup shredded Swiss cheese

1. Place the tortilla on a work surface and lay the ham over the bottom half of the tortilla. Top the ham with the bell pepper strips and the cheese. Fold the top half of the tortilla over the filling to make a half-moon. Press lightly to adhere.

2. Coat a medium nonstick skillet with cooking spray and heat over medium-low heat. Add the quesadilla and cook for 4 minutes, turning once, or until browned and the cheese melts. Cut into 3 wedges.

Per serving: 187 calories ▸ 18 g protein ▸ 14 g carbohydrates ▸ 10 g fat ▸ 5 g saturated fat ▸ 8 g fiber ▸ 437 mg sodium

GARDEN WRAP

With low-carb tortillas, you can enjoy a wrap without excessive carbohydrates that spike blood sugar. Be sure to read labels and select the brand with the lowest carb count per tortilla, usually around 7 grams.

Prep time: 10 minutes
Total time: 25 minutes
Makes 4 servings

- 1 tablespoon olive oil
- ½ red onion, thinly sliced
- ½ red bell pepper, thinly sliced
- 1 cup mushrooms, sliced
- ½ cup thawed frozen broccoli florets
- 4 cups baby arugula
- 8 eggs, lightly beaten
- ½ cup crumbled herb feta cheese
- 4 low-carb tortillas (7" diameter)

1. Warm the oil in a large nonstick skillet over medium-high heat. Cook the onion and bell pepper for 3 minutes, or until softened. Add the mushrooms and cook for 3 minutes, stirring occasionally, or until the mushrooms are tender. Add the broccoli and cook for 2 minutes, or until tender-crisp. Add the arugula and cook for 1 minute to wilt.

2. Add the eggs and reduce the heat to medium-low. Cook for 3 to 4 minutes, stirring, or until the eggs are softly scrambled but still moist and creamy. Stir in the cheese.

3. Place the tortillas on a flat surface. Divide the egg mixture among the tortillas, placing it on the bottom third of each. Fold in the sides and roll up burrito style. Cut in half with a serrated knife.

Per serving: 293 calories ▸ 22 g protein ▸ 15 g carbohydrates ▸ 20 g fat ▸ 6.5 g saturated fat ▸ 8 g fiber ▸ 359 mg sodium

BACON AND CHEESE BREAKFAST WRAP

Low-carb tortillas are soft right out of the package, so there is no need to heat as the filling will warm them. If you prefer them a little warmer, wrap the tortillas in paper towels and microwave on medium power for 30 seconds, or until warm.

Prep time: 15 minutes
Total time: 15 minutes
Makes 2 servings

1   small red onion, thinly sliced
3   cups baby spinach
4   slices Canadian bacon, chopped
½   teaspoon ground black pepper
2   ounces Jarlsberg cheese, shredded
2   low-carb tortillas (7" diameter)

1. Coat a medium nonstick skillet with cooking spray and heat over medium heat. Cook the onion for 5 minutes, stirring occasionally, or until browned. Add the spinach, bacon, and pepper and cook for 2 minutes, or until the spinach is wilted. Add the cheese and cook 1 minute, or until the cheese melts.

2. Place the tortillas on a flat surface. Divide the egg mixture among the tortillas, placing it on the bottom third of each. Fold in the sides and roll up burrito style. Cut in half with a serrated knife.

Per serving: 240 calories ▸ 23 g protein ▸ 19 g carbohydrates ▸ 12 g fat
▸ 5 g saturated fat ▸ 9 g fiber ▸ 765 mg sodium

LUNCHES

BURGERS WITH TZATZIKI SAUCE

Tzatziki is a traditional Greek cucumber-yogurt mixture that is used as a sauce or condiment. Brighten the flavor with the grated peel of 1 lemon and a few tablespoons of snipped fresh herbs, such as dill or mint. Serve this high-protein sauce as a sugar blocker.

Prep time: 15 minutes
Total time: 25 minutes
Makes 4 servings

1   pound extra-lean ground beef
1   cup (8 ounces) 2% plain Greek yogurt
1   small cucumber, peeled, seeded, grated, and excess liquid squeezed out
1   tablespoon fresh lemon juice
1   clove garlic, minced
½   teaspoon dried oregano
¼   teaspoon salt
1   tomato, sliced
1   small red onion, cut into ¼"-thick slices

1. Form the beef into 4 patties. Heat a large nonstick skillet coated with cooking spray over medium-high heat. Cook the burgers for 10 minutes, turning once, or until a thermometer inserted in the center registers 160°F.

2. Meanwhile, in a medium bowl, combine the yogurt, cucumber, lemon juice, garlic, oregano, and salt.

3. Place the burgers on each of 4 plates. Divide the tomato and onion among the burgers and serve with the tzatziki sauce.

Per serving: 207 calories ▶ 30 g protein ▶ 5 g carbohydrates ▶ 7 g fat ▶ 3 g saturated fat ▶ 1 g fiber ▶ 242 mg sodium

MUSHROOM TURKEY BURGERS

You can still enjoy burgers while limiting your carb intake. These burgers are stuffed with a moist and juicy mushroom filling. And since lettuce mimics the starch, you'll never miss the bun.

Prep time: 10 minutes
Total time: 30 minutes
Makes 4 servings

2   tablespoons olive oil, divided
4   ounces chopped mushrooms
1   small onion, finely chopped
1   clove garlic, minced
½   teaspoon salt, divided
¼   teaspoon dried thyme
1   pound lean ground turkey
4   leaves green leaf lettuce
¼   cup horseradish sauce sandwich spread

1. Warm 1 tablespoon of the oil in a large nonstick skillet over medium-high heat. Cook the mushrooms, onion, garlic, ¼ teaspoon of the salt, and the thyme for 6 minutes, stirring occasionally, or until lightly browned. Transfer the mushroom mixture to a small bowl and let cool 5 minutes. Wipe the skillet clean.

2. Shape the turkey into 4 balls. Make a well in the center of each ball and stuff with one-fourth of the cooled mushroom mixture. Pinch the turkey to seal in the filling and gently flatten into 3½" patties. Sprinkle the patties with the remaining ¼ teaspoon salt.

3. Warm the remaining 1 tablespoon oil in the same skillet over medium heat. Cook the patties for 12 minutes, turning once, or until cooked through.

4. Place 1 lettuce leaf on each of 4 plates and top each with a burger and 1 tablespoon of the horseradish sauce. Wrap the lettuce around the burgers to eat.

Per serving: 259 calories ▸ 24 g protein ▸ 6 g carbohydrates ▸ 16 g fat ▸ 4 g saturated fat ▸ 1 g fiber ▸ 539 mg sodium

DELUXE HAM PANINI

A panini press or grill pan will give nice markings to the sandwiches, but a regular nonstick or a cast-iron skillet will work just as well.

Prep time: 15 minutes
Total time: 25 minutes
Makes 4 servings

- 1 tablespoon olive oil
- 1 small sweet onion, thinly sliced
- 1 cup sliced mushrooms
- 4 low-carb tortillas (7" diameter)
- ¾ pound thinly sliced low-sodium deli ham
- ½ cup shredded reduced-fat, low-sodium Swiss cheese
- 1 cup prepared guacamole

1. Warm the oil in a large nonstick skillet over medium-high heat. Cook the onion and mushrooms for 5 minutes, stirring occasionally, or until lightly browned. Transfer the mushroom mixture to a bowl. Wipe the skillet clean.

2. Place the tortillas on a work surface. Evenly layer the ham and cheese down the center. Top with the mushroom mixture. Fold the short sides over the filling, then roll up burrito style to enclose the filling.

3. Coat the same skillet with cooking spray and heat over medium heat. Coat the top of each tortilla with cooking spray and place sprayed side down in the skillet. Place a heavy pan on top of the sandwiches. Cook for 2 minutes, or until lightly browned. Flip and cook for 2 minutes, or until lightly browned and the cheese is melted.

4. Place 1 pannini on each plate with ¼ cup guacamole.

....

Per serving: 387 calories ▶ 31 g protein ▶ 17 g carbohydrates ▶ 24 g fat ▶ 10 g saturated fat ▶ 7 g fiber ▶ 1,033 mg sodium

SMOKED TURKEY WRAPS

If you prefer a little heat, add 1 teaspoon chipotle
pepper sauce to the mayonnaise mixture.

Prep time: 15 minutes
Total time: 15 minutes
Makes 2 servings

1 tablespoon mayonnaise
1 tablespoon stone-ground mustard
2 low-carb tortillas (7" diameter)
½ cup baby spinach
3 ounces thinly sliced low-sodium deli smoked turkey breast
2 ounces thinly sliced Cheddar cheese
½ avocado, pitted, peeled, and thinly sliced
½ cup grape tomatoes, halved

1. In a cup, stir together the mayonnaise and mustard.
2. Place the tortillas on a work surface. Spread each with half of the mayonnaise mixture. Layer each with half the spinach, turkey, cheese, avocado, and tomatoes down the center. Fold the short sides over the filling, then roll up burrito style to enclose the filling. Cut each wrap in half and serve at once.

Per serving: 330 calories ► 23 g protein ► 21 g carbohydrates ► 22 g fat
► 8 g saturated fat ► 12 g fiber ► 783 mg sodium

CAESAR STEAK WRAP

This is a great way to use leftover cooked steak. You can also use strips of grilled chicken or turkey breast.

Prep time: 10 minutes
Total time: 15 minutes
Makes 1 serving

- 2 teaspoons mayonnaise
- ½ teaspoon Dijon mustard
- ½ teaspoon prepared horseradish
- 1 low-carb tortilla (7" diameter)
- 1 leaf romaine lettuce
- 2 ounces cooked lean steak, trimmed and thinly sliced
- ½ red bell pepper, cut into thin strips
- ½ rib celery, chopped
- 1 tablespoon grated Parmesan cheese

1. In a cup, stir together the mayonnaise, mustard, and horseradish.

2. Place the tortilla on a work surface and spread with the mayonnaise mixture. Layer the lettuce, steak, bell pepper, celery, and cheese down the center. Fold the short sides over the filling, then roll up burrito style to enclose the filling. Cut in half and serve at once.

Per serving: 242 calories ► 24 g protein ► 18 g carbohydrates ► 11 g fat ► 3 g saturated fat ► 10 g fiber ► 438 mg sodium

OPEN-FACED REUBEN

To save time, coleslaw mix may be substituted for the cabbage.

Prep time: 10 minutes
Total time: 15 minutes
Makes 1 serving

1   tablespoon reduced-fat mayonnaise
1   teaspoon white wine vinegar
⅛   teaspoon ground black pepper
½   cup shredded green cabbage
½   teaspoon mustard
1   slice whole wheat bread, toasted
2   ounces thinly sliced turkey pastrami
1   slice reduced-fat, low-sodium Swiss cheese

1. Preheat the broiler. Coat a broiler-pan rack with cooking spray.

2. In a medium bowl, whisk together the mayonnaise, vinegar, and pepper. Add the cabbage and toss to mix well.

3. Spread the mustard on the toast. Top with the pastrami, cabbage mixture, and cheese. Place on the broiler-pan rack and broil 5" from the heat for 2 minutes, or until the cheese is melted.

Per serving: 313 calories ▶ 21 g protein ▶ 17 g carbohydrates ▶ 17 g fat ▶ 7 g saturated fat ▶ 3 g fiber ▶ 802 mg sodium

TORTILLA PIZZAS

If you like, top the pizzas with 2 slices of crumbled crisp-cooked turkey bacon.

Prep time: 15 minutes
Total time: 30 minutes
Makes 2 servings

- 2 cups broccoli florets, coarsely chopped
- 2 low-carb tortillas (7" diameter)
- 4 tablespoons grated Parmesan cheese, divided
- 2 fully cooked chicken sausages (3 ounces each), cut into ½"-thick slices
- 2 plum tomatoes, chopped
- ½ cup shredded part-skim mozzarella cheese

1. Preheat the oven to 425°F.

2. In a medium microwaveable bowl, combine the broccoli and 2 tablespoons of water. Cover and microwave on high power for 2 minutes, or until the broccoli is tender-crisp. Drain and pat dry.

3. Place the tortillas on a baking sheet. Sprinkle each with 1 tablespoon of the Parmesan cheese. Top with the broccoli, sausages, and tomatoes. Top with the mozzarella and sprinkle each with 1 tablespoon of the remaining Parmesan cheese.

4. Bake for 10 minutes, or until the filling is hot and the cheese is melted. To serve, cut each pizza into 4 wedges.

Per serving: 350 calories ▸ 34 g protein ▸ 20 g carbohydrates ▸ 18 g fat ▸ 7g saturated fat ▸ 10 g fiber ▸ 805 mg sodium

SALMON STACKS

If you prefer, cook the patties on the stovetop in a nonstick skillet coated with cooking spray for 6 minutes, turning once, or until heated through. Transfer the patties to a plate and keep warm. Cook the onion and 2 teaspoons of oil in the same skillet for 5 minutes, or until softened.

Prep time: 10 minutes
Total time: 30 minutes
Makes 4 servings

1   can (14.75 ounces) salmon, drained and flaked
¼   cup golden flaxseed meal
¼   cup mayonnaise
1   large egg
2   tablespoons chopped fresh cilantro
1   tablespoon fresh lime juice
1   large onion, cut into 4 thick slices
1   large tomato, cut into 4 thick slices
4   tablespoons mild salsa
4   teaspoons 2% plain Greek yogurt

1. Preheat the oven to 375°F. Coat a large baking sheet with cooking spray.

2. In a medium bowl, combine the salmon, flaxseed meal, mayonnaise, egg, cilantro, and lime juice until well mixed. Shape the mixture into four 3" patties.

3. Place the patties on one side of the baking sheet. Place the onion slices on the other side of the baking sheet. Lightly coat the patties and onion with cooking spray. Bake for 20 minutes, turning the patties once, or until heated through and the onion is lightly browned.

4. Place a salmon patty on each of 4 plates. Top evenly with the onion, tomato, 1 table-spoon salsa, and 1 teaspoon yogurt.

Per serving: 291 calories ► 22 g protein ► 9 g carbohydrates ► 19 g fat ► 3 g saturated fat ► 3 g fiber ► 491 mg sodium

OPEN-FACED STEAK SANDWICHES

Other cuts of beef such as sirloin or New York strip may be used. Just make sure they are of the same thickness.

Prep time: 15 minutes
Total time: 35 minutes
Makes 4 servings

- 3 tablespoons olive oil
- 1 red onion, chopped
- 1½ cups grape tomatoes, halved
- 1 fresh jalapeño chile pepper, seeded and finely chopped (wear plastic gloves when handling)
- 2 tablespoons apple cider vinegar
- 1 clove garlic, chopped
- ½ teaspoon salt, divided
- ¼ cup chopped fresh cilantro
- 1 pound top round steak
- ¼ teaspoon ground black pepper
- 4 slices whole grain sourdough bread, toasted

1. Warm the oil in a large nonstick skillet over medium-high heat. Cook the onion for 5 minutes, stirring occasionally, or until soft and lightly browned. Add the tomatoes and jalapeño and cook for 2 minutes, stirring, or until the tomatoes begin to soften. Add the vinegar, garlic, and ¼ teaspoon of the salt. Cook for 5 minutes, stirring occasionally, or until the flavors are blended and the sauce has begun to thicken slightly. Remove from the heat. Stir in the cilantro.

2. Coat a small nonstick skillet with cooking spray and heat over medium-high heat. Sprinkle the steak with the pepper and remaining ¼ teaspoon salt. Cook the steak for 10 minutes, turning once, or until an instant-read thermometer inserted into the center registers 145°F for medium-rare. Transfer the steak to a cutting board and let stand for 5 minutes before thinly slicing across the grain.

3. Place the toast slices on a work surface. Top each with one-fourth of the steak and one-fourth of the tomato mixture.

Per serving: 413 calories ▶ 40 g protein ▶ 19 g carbohydrates ▶ 18 g fat ▶ 4 g saturated fat ▶ 3 g fiber ▶ 492 mg sodium

BLT SANDWICH

The protein in the bacon and the fat in the mayon-naise all work as sugar blockers against the bread. Be sure to use thin-sliced whole wheat bread with 7 or fewer carb grams per slice.

Prep time: 5 minutes
Total time: 5 minutes
Makes 1 serving

1   tablespoon mayonnaise
2   slices thin-sliced whole wheat bread, toasted
2   leaves Boston lettuce
2   slices tomato
3   slices crisp-cooked bacon

Spread the mayonnaise on 1 piece of toast. Top with the lettuce, tomato, bacon, and remaining toast. Cut in half to serve.

Per serving: 319 calories ▶ 12 g protein ▶ 16 g carbohydrates ▶ 22 g fat ▶ 5 g saturated fat ▶ 3 g fiber ▶ 795 mg sodium

TROPICAL ROAST BEEF WRAPS

To make ahead, place the assembled wraps on a plate, cover with a damp paper towel, and wrap tightly in plastic wrap. The sandwiches will keep in the refrigerator for up to 4 hours.

Prep time: 10 minutes
Total time: 15 minutes
Makes 2 servings

- 2 tablespoons reduced-fat mayonnaise
- ½ teaspoon curry powder
- ⅛ teaspoon salt
- ¼ pound thinly sliced low-sodium deli roast beef, coarsely chopped
- ¼ cup shredded Cheddar cheese
- 1 rib celery, chopped
- ½ fresh jalapeño chile pepper, seeded and finely chopped (wear plastic gloves when handling)
- 2 low-carb tortillas (7" diameter)
- 1 tablespoon mango chutney
- 2 leaves green leaf lettuce

1. In a large bowl, stir together the mayonnaise, curry powder, and salt. Add the roast beef, cheese, celery, and jalapeño. Toss to coat well.

2. Place the tortillas on a work surface. Spread each with half of the chutney. Evenly layer the lettuce, roast beef mixture, and mango down the center of each tortilla. Fold the short sides over the filling, then roll up burrito style to enclose the filling. Cut each wrap in half and serve at once.

Per serving: 315 calories ▶ 24 g protein ▶ 21 g carbohydrates ▶ 17 g fat ▶ 7 g saturated fat ▶ 8 g fiber ▶ 521 mg sodium

CUBANO SANDWICH

Serve this toasty sandwich with a sugar-blocking avocado half, cut into wedges and sprinkled with a little lime juice.

Prep time: 5 minutes
Total time: 15 minutes
Makes 1 serving

1½ teaspoons yellow mustard
2   slices high-fiber, low-carb whole wheat bread
2   slices (½ ounce each) low-sodium deli ham
1   slice (1 ounce) deli smoked turkey breast
1   slice (¾ ounce) low-fat Swiss cheese
3   slices reduced-sodium dill sandwich pickles

1. Spread the mustard on 1 slice of bread. Layer with the ham, turkey, cheese, and pickles. Top with the remaining slice of bread.

2. Coat a nonstick ridged grill pan with cooking spray and heat over medium-high heat, or heat a panini sandwich maker according to the manufacturer's instructions. Grill the sandwich for 8 minutes, turning once, or until the bread is well marked and the cheese is melted.

Per serving: 218 calories ▶ 21 g protein ▶ 22 g carbohydrates ▶ 5 g fat ▶ 2 g saturated fat ▶ 2 g fiber ▶ 962 mg sodium

PICKLED GINGER AND SALMON SALAD SANDWICH

This sandwich would be equally delicious with leftover grilled salmon.

Prep time: 15 minutes
Total time: 20 minutes
Makes 4 servings

- ¼ cup mayonnaise
- ¼ cup (2 ounces) 0% plain Greek yogurt
- 2 tablespoons white wine vinegar
- ¼ teaspoon ground black pepper
- 1 can (14.75 ounces) salmon, drained and flaked
- 2 ribs celery, finely chopped
- 2 tablespoons pickled ginger, drained and finely chopped
- 2 scallions, finely chopped
- 4 slices multigrain bread
- ½ cucumber, thinly sliced
- 2 small tomatoes, chopped

1. In a medium bowl, whisk together the mayonnaise, yogurt, vinegar, and pepper. Add the salmon, celery, ginger, and scallions. Stir until combined.

2. Place the bread slices on a work surface. Top each with one-fourth of the cucumber slices, the salmon mixture, and tomatoes. Cut each in half to serve.

Per serving: 152 calories ▶ 6 g protein ▶ 17 g carbohydrates ▶ 7 g fat ▶ 2 g saturated fat ▶ 4 g fiber ▶ 339 mg sodium

HAWAIIAN CARROT SALAD

To save time, use a 16-ounce bag of baby-cut carrots instead.

Prep time: 15 minutes
Total time: 40 minutes
Makes 4 servings

1	bag (16 ounces) carrots, sliced
3	tablespoons olive oil, divided
1	teaspoon Sucanat
½	teaspoon salt, divided
4	boneless, skinless chicken breast halves
¼	teaspoon ground ginger
1	bag (10 ounces) chopped romaine lettuce
2	cups fresh pineapple chunks
½	small red onion, thinly sliced
2	tablespoons rice wine vinegar

1. Preheat the oven to 425°F. Coat a large roasting pan with cooking spray. Toss the carrots, 1 tablespoon of the oil, the Sucanat, and ¼ teaspoon of the salt in the pan until well coated. Move the carrots to one side of the pan. Place the chicken on the other side of the pan. Brush the chicken with 1 tablespoon of the oil and sprinkle with the ginger and the remaining ¼ teaspoon salt.

2. Roast for 25 minutes, or until the carrots are tender and a thermometer inserted into the thickest part of a breast registers 160°F. Transfer the chicken to a cutting board. Let stand for 5 minutes before cutting into thin slices. Let the carrots cool slightly.

3. Meanwhile, in a large bowl, toss together the lettuce, pineapple, onion, vinegar, and the remaining 1 tablespoon oil.

4. Add the cooled carrots to the bowl and stir to combine. Serve with the chicken.

Per serving: 354 calories ▶ 29 g protein ▶ 31 g carbohydrates ▶ 14 g fat ▶ 2 g saturated fat ▶ 8 g fiber ▶ 378 mg sodium

ORANGE-JICAMA CHICKEN SALAD

Adding chia seeds to vinaigrettes is a great way to get these sugar-blocking seeds into your meals. Be sure to let them sit for 5 minutes so they can thicken the vinaigrette slightly.

Prep time: 10 minutes
Total time: 10 minutes
Makes 4 servings

- ¼ cup red wine vinegar
- ¼ cup olive oil
- 2 tablespoons chia seeds
- 2 tablespoons Sucanat
- 4 cups baby arugula
- 2 cups shredded cooked chicken breast
- ½ small jicama, peeled and cut into matchsticks
- 2 oranges, peeled and sectioned

1. In a large bowl, combine the vinegar, oil, chia seeds, and Sucanat until blended. Let stand for 5 minutes, stirring occasionally, or until the dressing thickens slightly.

2. Add the arugula, chicken, jicama, and oranges. Toss to coat well.

Per serving: 430 calories ▶ 28 g protein ▶ 37 g carbohydrates ▶ 20 g fat ▶ 3 g saturated fat ▶ 14 g fiber ▶ 168 mg sodium

WARM GOAT CHEESE AND ARUGULA SALAD

Chia seeds are very rich in omega-3 fatty acids. Use them as you would flaxseeds: sprinkled on cereal, in baked goods, or in drinks. They make an excellent crunchy coating for the goat cheese. Chia seeds can be found in health food stores and in the natural foods sections of most supermarkets.

Prep time: 15 minutes
Total time: 25 minutes + chilling time
Makes 4 servings

- 1 large egg
- 2 tablespoons plain dried bread crumbs
- 1 tablespoon chia seeds
- 1 log (8 ounces) reduced-fat soft goat cheese
- 3 tablespoons white wine vinegar
- 1½ teaspoons Dijon mustard
- ¼ teaspoon salt
- ¼ teaspoon ground black pepper
- 3 tablespoons olive oil, divided
- 2 packages (5 ounces each) baby arugula
- 2 cups cherry tomatoes, halved

1. In a pie plate, lightly whisk the egg until blended. On a sheet of waxed paper, combine the bread crumbs and chia seeds until well mixed. Cut the goat cheese crosswise into four ¾"-thick rounds. Dip the goat cheese, 1 round at a time, into the egg, then into the crumb mixture, lightly pressing to adhere. Transfer the rounds to a plate. Cover and refrigerate for 15 minutes.

2. Meanwhile, in a large bowl, whisk together the vinegar, mustard, salt, and pepper. Whisk in 2 tablespoons of the oil until blended. Add the arugula and tomatoes. Toss gently to coat well.

3. Warm the remaining 1 tablespoon oil in a medium nonstick skillet over medium heat. Cook the cheese rounds for 3 to 5 minutes, turning once, or until golden and slightly soft in the center.

4. Divide the arugula mixture among 4 plates and top each with a cheese round.

Per serving: 420 calories ▸ 37 g protein ▸ 24 g carbohydrates ▸ 30 g fat ▸ 10 g saturated fat ▸ 10 g fiber ▸ 108 mg sodium

SHRIMP AND CUCUMBER SALAD

Grilled salmon is a delicious alternative to the shrimp.

Prep time: 15 minutes
Total time: 15 minutes
Makes 2 servings

2 tablespoons mayonnaise
2 tablespoons sour cream
2 tablespoons chopped fresh dill
1 tablespoon rice wine vinegar
¼ teaspoon salt
⅛ teaspoon ground black pepper
6 ounces cooked peeled and deveined shrimp, coarsely chopped
½ medium cucumber, peeled and thinly sliced
1 rib celery, thinly sliced
1 scallion, chopped
2 cups baby salad greens
1 tomato, cut into 4 slices

1. In a large bowl, whisk together the mayonnaise, sour cream, dill, vinegar, salt, and pepper. Add the shrimp, cucumber, celery, and scallion. Toss to mix well.

2. Divide the greens and tomato slices between 2 plates and top with the shrimp mixture.

Per serving: 249 calories ▸ 20 g protein ▸ 8 g carbohydrates ▸ 15 g fat ▸ 3 g saturated fat ▸ 3 g fiber ▸ 542 mg sodium

LENTIL TABBOULEH SALAD

Green lentils, also known as French lentils, are smaller than brown lentils. They may take a few minutes longer to cook than other lentils, but they hold their shape well. As with all lentils, be sure to rinse them and pick out any stones before using.

Prep time: 15 minutes
Total time: 35 minutes
Makes 4 servings

1   cup green lentils
3   tablespoons olive oil
2   tablespoons red wine vinegar
1   teaspoon grated lemon peel
½   teaspoon salt
¼   teaspoon ground black pepper
2   tomatoes, chopped
1   small cucumber, peeled, seeded, and chopped
2   scallions, finely chopped
½   cup chopped fresh parsley
¼   cup chopped fresh mint

1. In a large saucepan, bring 4 cups of water to a boil over high heat. Add the lentils and reduce to a simmer. Cover and cook for 20 minutes, or just until tender. Drain well and cool.

2. Meanwhile, in a large bowl, whisk together the oil, vinegar, lemon peel, salt, and pepper. Add the tomatoes, cucumber, scallions, parsley, and mint.

3. Add the cooled lentils and stir to combine well. Serve chilled or at room temperature.

Per serving: 278 calories ▶ 12 g protein ▶ 34 g carbohydrates ▶ 12 g fat ▶ 1.5 g saturated fat ▶ 10 g fiber ▶ 321 mg sodium

SUSHI SALAD

Nori are paper-thin sheets of dried seaweed, which is rich in protein, calcium, and iron. You can find nori in the Asian aisle of most supermarkets.

Prep time: 20 minutes
Total time: 30 minutes
Makes 4 servings

2   tablespoons reduced-sodium soy sauce
2   tablespoons rice wine vinegar
2   tablespoons pickled ginger, finely chopped
1   tablespoon toasted sesame oil
$\frac{1}{4}$ teaspoon salt
2   cups cooked brown rice
1   tomato, chopped
$\frac{1}{2}$ cucumber, peeled and cut into $\frac{1}{2}$" chunks
1   small carrot, grated
1   can (6 ounces) lump crabmeat, drained
1   Hass avocado, pitted, peeled, and cut into $\frac{1}{2}$" chunks
1   sheet nori, cut into thin strips

1. In a large bowl, whisk together the soy sauce, vinegar, ginger, sesame oil, and salt. Add the rice, tomato, cucumber, and carrot. Toss to coat well.

2. Divide the rice mixture among 4 plates. Top evenly with the crabmeat, avocado, and nori strips.

Per serving: 303 calories ▸ 15 g protein ▸ 33 g carbohydrates ▸ 12 g fat ▸ 1.5 g saturated fat ▸ 7 g fiber ▸ 656 mg sodium

CREAMY BROCCOLI-CARROT SALAD

Be sure not to overcook the broccoli for the best sugar-blocking effect. Dried cherries or golden raisins may be used in place of the cranberries, but be sure whichever you choose does not have added sugar.

Prep time: 15 minutes
Total time: 25 minutes
Makes 4 servings

- 4 cups broccoli florets
- ½ cup reduced-fat mayonnaise
- 2 tablespoons white wine vinegar
- 1 tablespoon chopped fresh dill
- ¼ teaspoon salt
- ⅛ teaspoon ground black pepper
- 2 cups chopped cooked chicken breast
- 1 small carrot, grated
- ½ cup walnuts, chopped
- ¼ cup dried cranberries
- 3 tablespoons minced red onion

1. Place a steamer basket in a large saucepan with 2″ of water. Bring to a boil, add the broccoli, and steam for 4 minutes, or until tender-crisp. Drain under cold running water and drain again.

2. In a large bowl, whisk together the mayonnaise, vinegar, dill, salt, and pepper. Add the chicken, carrot, walnuts, cranberries, onion, and the cooled broccoli. Toss to coat well.

Per serving: 294 calories ▸ 22 g protein ▸ 19 g carbohydrates ▸ 16 g fat ▸ 2 g saturated fat ▸ 4 g fiber ▸ 251 mg sodium

BARLEY AND SPINACH SALAD

If you like, use 1 cup whole wheat couscous instead of the barley, prepared according to package directions.

Prep time: 20 minutes
Total time: 35 minutes
Makes 4 servings

1   cup quick-cooking barley
3   tablespoons fresh lemon juice
2   tablespoons extra-virgin olive oil
½   teaspoon salt
¼   teaspoon ground black pepper
1   package (5 ounces) baby spinach
2   peaches, pitted and chopped
1   shallot, thinly sliced
½   cup Gorgonzola cheese, crumbled
2   slices (1 ounce each) prosciutto, cut into thin strips

1. In a large saucepan, bring 2 cups water to a boil over high heat. Add the barley and reduce to a simmer. Cover and cook for 10 minutes, or just until tender. Drain well and cool.

2. Meanwhile, in a large bowl, whisk together the lemon juice, oil, salt, and pepper. Add the spinach, peaches, and shallot, and toss to coat well.

3. Add the cooled barley to the bowl and toss again. Divide the salad among 4 plates and top each evenly with the Gorgonzola and prosciutto.

Per serving: 335 calories ▶ 15 g protein ▶ 40 g carbohydrates ▶ 15 g fat ▶ 5.5 g saturated fat ▶ 7 g fiber ▶ 994 mg sodium

VEGGIE BURGER SLAW

For the best flavor, follow the package directions for grilling the patties.

Prep time: 20 minutes
Total time: 30 minutes
Makes 4 servings

- 1 package (9.5 ounces) garden vegetable patties
- 2 tablespoons apple cider vinegar
- 2 tablespoons canola oil
- 3-4 drops hot sauce
- 1/4 teaspoon salt
- 1/2 package (16 ounces) coleslaw mix
- 2 tomatoes, chopped
- 3 ounces pepper Jack cheese, cut into 1/2" pieces
- 1/4 cup chopped fresh cilantro
- 2 scallions, thinly sliced

1. Prepare the patties according to package directions. Let cool, then cut into 1/2"-wide strips.

2. In a large bowl, whisk together the vinegar, oil, hot sauce, and salt. Add the coleslaw, tomatoes, cheese, cilantro, scallions, and the cooled patty strips. Toss to coat well.

Per serving: 320 calories ▶ 22 g protein ▶ 15 g carbohydrates ▶ 20 g fat ▶ 5.5 g saturated fat ▶ 6 g fiber ▶ 702 mg sodium

MEXICALI SALAD

To make homemade tortilla strips, coat 2 corn tortillas (6″ diameter) with cooking spray. Heat in a small nonstick skillet over medium-low heat for 4 minutes, turning once, or until browned in spots and crisp. Cut each tortilla crosswise into thin strips.

Prep time: 15 minutes
Total time: 15 minutes
Makes 4 servings

¼ cup mild or medium salsa
    Grated peel and juice of 1 lime
1   tablespoon olive oil
¼   teaspoon salt
1   can (14–19 ounces) black beans, rinsed and drained
1   zucchini, cut into ½″ cubes
1   Hass avocado, pitted, peeled, and cut into 1″ chunks
½   cup fresh or frozen and thawed corn kernels
2   scallions, thinly sliced
½   package (3.5 ounces) tortilla strips

In a large bowl, stir together the salsa, lime peel, lime juice, oil, and salt until blended. Add the beans, zucchini, avocado, corn, and scallions. Toss to coat well. Serve topped with the tortilla strips.

Per serving: 233 calories ▸ 7 g protein ▸ 28 g carbohydrates ▸ 11 g fat ▸ 1.5 g saturated fat ▸ 7 g fiber ▸ 560 mg sodium

SOBA NOODLE SALAD

Buckwheat noodles cook quickly—usually in about 4 minutes. Be careful not to overcook them or they can become limp and mushy.

Prep time: 20 minutes
Total time: 30 minutes
Makes 4 servings

- 6 ounces buckwheat (soba) noodles
- 3 ounces sugar snap peas, strings removed
- 2 cups sliced cooked chicken breast
- 4 radishes, thinly sliced
- 2 scallions, thinly sliced
- ½ cup Asian-style salad dressing
- 4 teaspoons sesame seeds, toasted

1. Bring a large pot of water to a boil. Add the noodles and cook according to package directions. Add the snap peas during the last 2 minutes of cooking. Drain, rinse under cold water, and drain again. Transfer to a large bowl.

2. Add the chicken, radishes, scallions, and dressing. Toss to coat well. Serve sprinkled with the sesame seeds.

Per serving: 337 calories ▸ 30 g protein ▸ 44 g carbohydrates ▸ 4 g fat ▸ 1 g saturated fat ▸ 2 g fiber ▸ 759 mg sodium

COUSCOUS, SHRIMP, AND CHICKPEA SALAD

Chia seeds nicely thicken the dressing. If you prefer to make this vegetarian, swap out the shrimp for chopped baked tofu instead.

Prep time: 15 minutes
Total time: 15 minutes
Makes 4 servings

1 tablespoon chia seeds
¾ cup whole wheat couscous
¾ cup boiling water
½ pound cooked peeled and deveined shrimp, halved lengthwise
1 cup canned chickpeas, rinsed and drained
1 zucchini, chopped
4 scallions, chopped
¼ cup chopped fresh mint
⅓ cup red wine vinaigrette
3 tablespoons red wine vinegar

1. In a small bowl, combine the chia seeds and ¼ cup water. Let stand for 10 minutes, stirring occasionally, or until the mixture is thickened and of a gel-like consistency.

2. Meanwhile, combine the couscous and boiling water in a large bowl. Cover and let stand for 5 minutes, then fluff with a fork.

3. Add the shrimp, chickpeas, zucchini, scallions, mint, vinaigrette, vinegar, and the chia seed mixture and toss to coat well.

Per serving: 304 calories ▸ 20 g protein ▸ 37 g carbohydrates ▸ 9 g fat ▸ 1 g saturated fat ▸ 9 g fiber ▸ 356 mg sodium

GREEK SALAD–STUFFED TOMATOES

The perfect summer lunch, this chickpea-studded salad is a delicious twist on a Greek salad. For a change of pace, serve over a bed of greens.

Prep time: 20 minutes
Total time: 25 minutes
Makes 4 servings

- 4 large tomatoes
- ½ cup red wine vinegar
- 2 tablespoons extra-virgin olive oil
- 1 teaspoon salt-free garlic-herb seasoning blend
- 1 teaspoon dried oregano
- 1 can (15 ounces) chickpeas, rinsed and drained
- ½ cucumber, peeled, seeded, and chopped
- ½ green bell pepper, chopped
- ¼ cup chopped pitted kalamata olives
- ¼ cup reduced-fat feta cheese crumbles

1. Cut a ½" slice off the stem end of each tomato. With a small spoon, gently scoop out and discard the pulp to create a hollow shell. Turn the tomatoes upside down on a large plate lined with paper towels and let drain for 5 minutes.

2. Meanwhile, in a large bowl, whisk together the vinegar, oil, seasoning blend, and oregano. Add the chickpeas, cucumber, bell pepper, olives, and cheese. Gently toss to coat well.

3. Spoon the chickpea mixture into the tomato shells and serve.

Per serving: 241 calories ▸ 9 g protein ▸ 27 g carbohydrates ▸ 12 g fat ▸ 2.5 g saturated fat ▸ 6 g fiber ▸ 609 mg sodium

FIRST COURSES

CHEESY ZUCCHINI STICKS

To make your own blue cheese dressing, stir 2 table-spoons crumbled blue cheese into ⅓ cup of plain Greek yogurt or reduced-fat mayonnaise.

Prep time: 15 minutes
Total time: 30 minutes
Makes 4 servings

---

1 large egg
1 tablespoon water
2 medium zucchini, cut into 4" × ½" sticks
⅓ cup grated Parmesan cheese
3 tablespoons almond flour
1 tablespoon whole wheat pastry flour
1 tablespoon chia seeds
1½ teaspoons salt-free lemon-pepper seasoning
  Pinch of salt
⅓ cup blue cheese or ranch dressing

1. Preheat the oven to 450°F. Coat a large baking sheet with cooking spray.

2. In a large bowl, whisk together the egg and water until frothy. Add the zucchini, tossing to coat well. Combine the cheese, almond flour, pastry flour, chia seeds, lemon-pepper seasoning, and salt in a large resealable food storage bag. Add the zucchini in batches, shaking the bag to coat all sides.

3. Arrange the zucchini in one layer on the baking sheet. Lightly coat the zucchini with cooking spray. Bake for 15 minutes, or until crisp and golden. Serve with the dressing.

....

Per serving: 215 calories ▶ 8 g protein ▶ 9 g carbohydrates ▶ 17 g fat ▶ 4 g saturated fat ▶ 3 g fiber ▶ 390 mg sodium

SHRIMP CRACKERS WITH WASABI CREAM CHEESE

Rice crackers are gluten-free crackers made from almonds and rice flour. They can be found in the Asian section of most supermarkets.

Prep time: 15 minutes
Total time: 25 minutes
Makes 4 servings

3 ounces cream cheese, at room temperature
½ teaspoon reduced-sodium soy sauce
½ teaspoon wasabi paste
24 rice crackers
24 cooked peeled and deveined medium shrimp
1 scallion, finely chopped

1. In a small bowl, combine the cream cheese, soy sauce, and wasabi paste until blended.

2. Spread each cracker with some of the cream cheese mixture, top each with 1 shrimp, and sprinkle with the scallion.

Per serving: 163 calories ► 10 g protein ► 11 g carbohydrates ► 9 g fat ► 4 g saturated fat ► 0 g fiber ► 200 mg sodium

AVOCADO-TUNA DIP

Serve this dip with colorful strips of bell peppers and halved cherry tomatoes.

Prep time: 10 minutes
Total time: 15 minutes + chilling time
Makes 6 servings (1½ cups)

1   Hass avocado, pitted, peeled, and cut into 4 pieces
¼   cup light mayonnaise
1   scallion, cut into 1" pieces
2   tablespoons fresh lemon juice
¼   teaspoon salt
1   can (5 ounces) olive oil-packed chunk light tuna, drained

In a food processor, puree the avocado, mayonnaise, scallion, lemon juice, and salt. Add the tuna and pulse until smooth. Transfer to a bowl. Cover and refrigerate at least 1 hour to allow the flavors to blend.

Per serving: 135 calories ▶ 8 g protein ▶ 4 g carbohydrates ▶ 10 g fat ▶ 1.5 g saturated fat ▶ 2 g fiber ▶ 251 mg sodium

SMOKED SALMON DIP

For an elegant presentation, spoon the mixture onto thick slices of cucumber and garnish with fresh dill sprigs.

Prep time: 10 minutes
Total time: 15 minutes + chilling time
Makes 8 servings (2 cups)

4	ounces smoked salmon, finely chopped
1	cup 2% plain Greek yogurt
6	tablespoons sour cream
2	tablespoons capers, drained and chopped
1½	teaspoons grated lemon peel
¾	teaspoon dried dillweed
3	drops hot sauce

In a medium bowl, combine the salmon, yogurt, sour cream, capers, lemon peel, dillweed, and hot sauce until blended. Cover and refrigerate for 1 hour to allow the flavors to blend.

Per serving: 86 calories ▸ 11 g protein ▸ 2 g carbohydrates ▸ 4 g fat ▸ 2 g saturated fat ▸ 0 g fiber ▸ 109 mg sodium

MEDITERRANEAN ALMOND DIP

Stock up on precut vegetables such as carrots, bell peppers, mushrooms, and broccoli florets. Use them throughout the week with a dip for snacks, or in stir-fries, soups, and salads.

Prep time: 15 minutes
Total time: 20 minutes
Makes 8 servings (2 cups)

½ cup blanched whole almonds, toasted
½ cup loosely packed fresh flat-leaf parsley
3 scallions, cut into 1" pieces
1 can (15 ounces) chickpeas, rinsed and drained
¾ cup roasted red pepper strips, drained
¼ cup water
2 tablespoons olive oil
2 tablespoons white wine vinegar
½ teaspoon salt
⅛ teaspoon ground red pepper
Assorted vegetables (such as carrot sticks, celery sticks, and bell pepper strips)

In a food processor, pulse the almonds, parsley, and scallions until coarsely ground. Add the chickpeas, red pepper strips, water, oil, vinegar, salt, and ground red pepper and puree. Transfer to a bowl. Serve with the vegetables.

Per serving: 129 calories ▶ 4 g protein ▶ 11 g carbohydrates ▶ 8 g fat ▶ 1 g saturated fat ▶ 2 g fiber ▶ 192 mg sodium

RED PEPPER AND FETA SPREAD

Serve this spread on cucumber slices or toasted pita wedges. It's also delicious as a sandwich spread.

Prep time: 15 minutes
Total time: 30 minutes + chilling time
Makes 6 servings (1½ cups)

- 3 tablespoons olive oil, divided
- ¼ red onion, finely chopped
- 2 cloves garlic, minced
- ½ teaspoon red-pepper flakes
- 1 jar (12 ounces) roasted red peppers, rinsed and drained
- 4 ounces feta cheese, crumbled
- 2 tablespoons red wine vinegar
- ½ teaspoon salt

1. Heat 1 tablespoon of the oil in a small nonstick skillet over medium-low heat. Cook the onion, garlic, and red-pepper flakes for 5 minutes, stirring occasionally, or until the onion is soft. Remove from the heat and let cool for 5 minutes.

2. In a food processor, pulse the roasted peppers until coarsely chopped. Add the onion mixture, cheese, vinegar, salt, and the remaining 2 tablespoons oil and puree. Cover and refrigerate at least 1 hour to allow the flavors to blend.

Per serving: 127 calories ▶ 3 g protein ▶ 5 g carbohydrates ▶ 11 g fat ▶ 4 g saturated fat ▶ 1 g fiber ▶ 441 mg sodium

ROAST ASPARAGUS WITH FETA AND LEMON

You can add a handful of grape or cherry tomatoes to the pan after the asparagus has roasted for 5 minutes.

Prep time: 10 minutes
Total time: 20 minutes
Makes 4 servings

1   pound asparagus
2   tablespoons olive oil, divided
    Grated peel and juice of 1 lemon
¼   teaspoon salt
⅛   teaspoon ground black pepper
1   ounce feta cheese, crumbled
3   tablespoons pine nuts, toasted

1. Preheat the oven to 425°F. In a small shallow roasting pan, toss the asparagus with 1 tablespoon of the oil. Roast for 8 minutes, tossing occasionally, or until tender-crisp.

2. Meanwhile, in a small bowl, whisk together the lemon peel, lemon juice, salt, pepper, and the remaining 1 tablespoon oil until blended.

3. Transfer the asparagus to a platter. Drizzle with the dressing. Top with the cheese and sprinkle with the pine nuts.

Per serving: 185 calories ▶ 5 g protein ▶ 7 g carbohydrates ▶ 17 g fat ▶ 3 g saturated fat ▶ 3 g fiber ▶ 302 mg sodium

WALNUT AND BLUE CHEESE BALL

Instead of the same old crackers and chips, try "super scoopers" like endive spears, wedges of fennel, and thick slices of cucumber rounds.

Prep time: 20 minutes
Total time: 30 minutes + chilling time
Makes 16 servings (2 cups)

1⅓ cups toasted walnuts, divided
6 ounces cream cheese, at room temperature
4 ounces blue cheese, crumbled
6 dried apricot halves, coarsely chopped
2 tablespoons mayonnaise
1 scallion, coarsely chopped
1 teaspoon apple cider vinegar
½ teaspoon Worcestershire sauce

1. In a food processor, pulse the walnuts 10 seconds or until coarsely ground. Transfer 1 cup of the ground nuts to a small bowl; set aside.

2. Add the cream cheese, blue cheese, apricots, mayonnaise, scallion, vinegar, and Worcestershire to the food processor and pulse 1 minute or until blended.

3. Scrape the cheese mixture onto a large sheet of plastic wrap. Form into a ball with a rubber spatula. Wrap the cheese ball in plastic wrap and refrigerate for at least 2 hours or up to overnight.

4. Place the reserved 1 cup chopped nuts on a sheet of waxed paper. Unwrap the cheese ball and gently roll in the chopped nuts, turning to coat well. Place on a serving plate. Serve immediately, or cover and refrigerate until ready to serve.

Per serving: 250 calories ▸ 8 g protein ▸ 7 g carbohydrates ▸ 22 g fat ▸ 6.5 g saturated fat ▸ 2 g fiber ▸ 365 mg sodium

MARINATED CAULIFLOWER WITH OLIVES

Add 2 cups cooked broccoli florets to the cauliflower if you like.

Prep time: 15 minutes
Total time: 25 minutes + chilling time
Makes 4 servings (5 cups)

1   medium head cauliflower, cut into florets
¼   cup distilled white vinegar
3   tablespoons olive oil
1   clove garlic, minced
¼   teaspoon salt
¼   teaspoon ground black pepper
1   cup chopped fresh basil
½   cup pitted marinated olives, drained and coarsely chopped

1. Bring a large pot of water to a boil. Cook the cauliflower for 3 minutes, or until tender-crisp. Drain.

2. Meanwhile, in a large bowl, whisk together the vinegar, oil, garlic, salt, and pepper. Stir in the basil and olives.

3. Add the cauliflower to the dressing and toss to coat well. Cover and refrigerate 1 hour to allow the flavors to blend.

Per serving: 166 calories ► 3 g protein ► 9 g carbohydrates ► 14 g fat ► 1.5 g saturated fat ► 3 g fiber ► 500 mg sodium

CHEDDAR-BACON CRACKERS

Store the crackers in an airtight container at room temperature for up to 2 weeks.

Prep time: 30 minutes
Total time: 1 hour
Makes 18 servings (4½ dozen)

¼ cup 1% milk
1 large egg
½ cup old-fashioned rolled oats
¾ cup whole wheat pastry flour
½ teaspoon baking powder
¼ teaspoon ground red pepper
¼ teaspoon salt
1 cup shredded sharp Cheddar cheese
3 tablespoons cold butter, cut into small pieces
4 slices crisp-cooked bacon, crumbled
2 teaspoons chia seeds
2 teaspoons sesame seeds

1. In a small bowl, whisk together the milk and egg until blended. Stir in the oats until well mixed. Let stand 10 minutes.

2. In a food processor, combine the flour, baking powder, ground red pepper, and salt and pulse until blended. Add the cheese and butter and pulse until the mixture resembles coarse crumbs. Add the oat mixture and bacon and pulse just until the mixture begins to form a soft dough.

3. Divide the dough in half. Shape each half into a disk and wrap in plastic wrap. Refrigerate for 30 minutes.

4. Preheat the oven to 350°F. Line 2 large baking sheets with parchment paper or coat with cooking spray.

5. On a lightly floured surface, with a lightly floured rolling pin, roll out one disk of the dough to a ⅛" thickness. Sprinkle the dough with 1 teaspoon each of the chia seeds and sesame seeds. With a rolling pin, gently press the seeds into the dough. With a fluted pastry cutter or sharp knife, cut the dough into 2" squares. Place the squares ½" apart on a baking sheet. Repeat with the remaining dough, chia seeds, and sesame seeds.

6. Bake for 15 minutes, or until the crackers are golden brown, rotating the baking sheets halfway through baking. Let cool on the baking sheets on racks for 1 minute. With a spatula, transfer the crackers to racks to cool completely.

Per serving: 108 calories ▶ 4 g protein ▶ 5 g carbohydrates ▶ 8 g fat ▶ 3 g saturated fat ▶ 1 g fiber ▶ 165 mg sodium

ALMOND CHEESE CRISPS

Ground flaxseeds add lots of fiber and a nutty flavor to these light and crunchy snacks. Store them at room temperature between layers of waxed paper in an airtight container for up to 3 days.

Prep time: 10 minutes
Total time: 20 minutes
Makes 4 servings (12 crisps)

½ cup shredded Parmesan cheese
½ cup shredded mozzarella-provolone cheese blend
1   tablespoon ground flaxseeds
¼ cup sliced almonds

1. Preheat the oven to 400°F. Line a large baking sheet with parchment paper or a nonstick liner. In a medium bowl, combine the Parmesan cheese, mozzarella blend, flaxseeds, and almonds until blended.

2. Using your fingers, form 12 small piles of the Parmesan mixture 2" apart on the prepared baking sheet. Flatten each mound slightly into a 2" round. Bake for 10 minutes, or until the edges are lightly browned. Cool on the baking sheet for 2 minutes. With a small metal spatula, carefully transfer the crisps to a rack to cool completely.

Per serving: 132 calories ▶ 8 g protein ▶ 2 g carbohydrates ▶ 10 g fat ▶ 4 g saturated fat ▶ 1 g fiber ▶ 239 mg sodium

SPICY MEXICAN PEANUTS

These addictive spicy nuts are superfast to make and the perfect finger food. Serve them warm or at room temperature.

Prep time: 5 minutes
Total time: 10 minutes
Makes 8 servings (2 cups)

1   teaspoon chili powder
1   teaspoon ground cumin
½   teaspoon kosher salt
¼   teaspoon ground ginger
¼   teaspoon ground red pepper
1   tablespoon olive oil
1   clove garlic, minced
2   cups unsalted dry-roasted peanuts

1. In a cup, mix together the chili powder, cumin, salt, ginger, and ground red pepper until well mixed.

2. Warm the oil in a large skillet over medium heat. Cook the garlic for 1 minute, stirring constantly, or until fragrant. Add the peanuts and the chili mixture and cook, shaking the skillet occasionally, for 1 to 2 minutes, or until the peanuts are well coated. Let cool completely.

Per serving: 232 calories ▶ 9 g protein ▶ 8 g carbohydrates ▶ 20 g fat ▶ 3 g saturated fat ▶ 3 g fiber ▶ 126 mg sodium

ASIAN TURKEY LETTUCE CUPS

For added crunch, stir ¼ pound of sliced snow peas into the turkey mixture in step 2.

Prep time: 15 minutes
Total time: 25 minutes
Makes 4 servings

- ¾ pound ground turkey
- 2 cloves garlic, minced
- ¼ teaspoon red-pepper flakes
- ½ cup canned sliced water chestnuts, drained and chopped
- 3 tablespoons rice wine vinegar
- 3 tablespoons reduced-sodium soy sauce
- 4 teaspoons toasted sesame oil
- ¼ cup chopped fresh cilantro
- 2 scallions, thinly sliced
- 8 leaves green leaf lettuce
- ¼ cup dry-roasted peanuts, chopped

1. Coat a large nonstick skillet with cooking spray and set over medium-high heat. Cook the turkey, garlic, and red-pepper flakes for 5 minutes, breaking up the meat with a wooden spoon, or until no longer pink.

2. Add the water chestnuts, vinegar, soy sauce, and sesame oil. Reduce the heat to medium and cook for 5 minutes, stirring occasionally, or until most of the liquid has evaporated. Remove from the heat and stir in the cilantro and scallions.

3. Divide the turkey mixture among the lettuce leaves and top with the peanuts.

Per serving: 247 calories ► 18 g protein ► 8 g carbohydrates ► 16 g fat ► 3 g saturated fat ► 2 g fiber ► 488 mg sodium

SOY-GLAZED WINGS

If using chicken wings instead of wingettes, cut off and discard the tips of the chicken wings, then cut the wings in half at the joint.

Prep time: 20 minutes
Total time: 45 minutes +
marinating time
Makes 8 servings

1/3 cup reduced-sodium soy sauce
4 tablespoons white wine vinegar, divided
1 tablespoon molasses
1 tablespoon Sriracha hot sauce
2 pounds wingettes or chicken wings
1 tablespoon hoisin sauce
1 tablespoon water
1 teaspoon toasted sesame oil
1 teaspoon grated fresh ginger

1. In a large resealable plastic food storage bag, combine the soy sauce, 3 tablespoons of the vinegar, the molasses, and Sriracha. Add the chicken, squeeze out the air, and seal the bag; turn to coat the chicken. Refrigerate, turning the bag occasionally, at least 2 hours or up to overnight.

2. Preheat the oven to 425°F. Line a baking sheet with foil and coat the foil with cooking spray. Place the chicken in a single layer on the baking sheet.

3. Roast for 20 to 25 minutes, turning occasionally, or until the chicken is browned, no longer pink inside, and the juices run clear.

4. Meanwhile, in a small bowl, whisk together the hoisin sauce, water, remaining 1 tablespoon vinegar, the sesame oil, and ginger. Serve as a dipping sauce with the chicken.

Per serving: 276 calories ▸ 21 g protein ▸ 4 g carbohydrates ▸ 19 g fat ▸ 5 g saturated fat ▸ 0 g fiber ▸ 509 mg sodium

CHICKEN NUGGETS WITH RÉMOULADE DIP

Serve the chicken nuggets with 2 cups of steamed broccoli florets sprinkled with lemon juice and a drizzle of olive oil.

Prep time: 20 minutes
Total time: 30 minutes
Makes 8 servings

- ⅓ cup mayonnaise
- 3 tablespoons ketchup
- 3 tablespoons stone-ground mustard
- 1 scallion, finely chopped
- 1½ teaspoons smoked paprika, divided
- 1 large egg
- 1 tablespoon water
- 1 pound chicken tenders, cut into 1" chunks
- ½ cup cornmeal
- ½ teaspoon salt
- ¼ teaspoon ground black pepper
- ½ cup canola oil

1. In a small bowl, combine the mayonnaise, ketchup, mustard, scallion, and ½ teaspoon of the paprika until blended. Set the rémoulade sauce aside.

2. In a large bowl, whisk the egg and water until frothy. Add the chicken, tossing to coat well. In a large resealable plastic food storage bag, combine the cornmeal, salt, pepper, and remaining 1 teaspoon paprika. Add the chicken and shake until well coated.

3. Warm the oil in a large nonstick skillet over medium-high heat. Working in batches, cook the chicken for 5 minutes, turning once, or until no longer pink and the juices run clear. Transfer to a paper towel–lined plate.

4. Serve the chicken with the rémoulade sauce as a dip.

Per serving: 383 calories ▶ 10 g protein ▶ 16 g carbohydrates ▶ 24 g fat ▶ 3.5 g saturated fat ▶ 1 g fiber ▶ 599 mg sodium

PICKLED SHRIMP WITH CREAMY COCKTAIL SAUCE

To keep the shrimp well chilled when serving, set the bowl of shrimp in a larger bowl of crushed ice.

Prep time: 10 minutes
Total time: 15 minutes + marinating time
Makes 6 servings

- ½ red onion, thinly sliced
- ¼ cup olive oil
- ¼ cup white wine vinegar
- ¼ teaspoon salt
- ¼ teaspoon ground black pepper
- 1 pound cooked peeled and deveined medium shrimp
- ½ cup cocktail sauce
- ¼ cup mayonnaise
- ¼ cup sour cream

1. In a large bowl, combine the onion, oil, vinegar, salt, and pepper. Add the shrimp, tossing to coat well. Cover and refrigerate at least 2 hours or overnight.

2. In a small bowl, whisk together the cocktail sauce, mayonnaise, and sour cream until blended.

3. Remove the shrimp from the marinade and transfer to a large serving bowl. Serve with the sauce.

Per serving: 266 calories ▶ 16 g protein ▶ 6 g carbohydrates ▶ 20 g fat ▶ 3.5 g saturated fat ▶ 1 g fiber ▶ 532 mg sodium

SPINACH, FETA, AND WALNUT SALAD

Serve this Mediterranean-inspired salad with a few stuffed grape leaves on the side.

Prep time: 10 minutes
Total time: 20 minutes
Makes 4 servings

- 2 tablespoons red wine vinegar
- 1 tablespoon extra-virgin olive oil
- ¼ teaspoon salt
- ¼ teaspoon ground black pepper
- 1 container (5 ounces) baby spinach
- 2 ribs celery, thinly sliced
- 1 cup roasted red pepper strips, drained
- ½ cup walnuts, toasted and coarsely chopped
- ⅓ cup crumbled feta cheese

1. In a large bowl, whisk together the vinegar, oil, salt, and black pepper. Add the spinach and celery, tossing to coat well.

2. Divide the spinach mixture among 4 plates. Top with the roasted pepper strips, walnuts, and cheese.

Per serving: 212 calories ▶ 5 g protein ▶ 12 g carbohydrates ▶ 17 g fat ▶ 3 g saturated fat ▶ 3 g fiber ▶ 752 mg sodium

WATERMELON SALAD

Choose smaller seedless watermelons, often called mini or baby melons. They are sweeter, have a thin rind, are easier to cut, and take up very little space in the refrigerator. For the best flavor, serve the salad chilled.

Prep time: 10 minutes
Total time: 15 minutes
Makes 4 servings

2 tablespoons fresh lemon juice
2 tablespoons olive oil
¼ teaspoon salt
⅛ teaspoon ground red pepper
3 cups cubed watermelon
3 small red or yellow tomatoes, cut into wedges
⅓ cup chopped fresh basil
3 tablespoons crumbled Gorgonzola cheese

1. In a large bowl, whisk together the lemon juice, oil, salt, and ground red pepper.

2. Add the watermelon, tomatoes, and basil, and toss gently to coat well. Sprinkle with the cheese.

Per serving: 136 calories ▸ 3 g protein ▸ 12 g carbohydrates ▸ 10 g fat ▸ 2.5 g saturated fat ▸ 2 g fiber ▸ 251 mg sodium

HOT AND SOUR SLAW

If you like, use Savoy cabbage in place of the green cabbage. It has a milder flavor and a more delicate texture.

Prep time: 10 minutes
Total time: 45 minutes
Makes 6 servings

2   slices bacon, cut crosswise into $1/4$" pieces
1   sweet onion, thinly sliced
$1/2$ head green cabbage, shredded
$1/2$ cup water
$1/4$ cup apple cider vinegar
$3/4$ teaspoon salt
$1/4$ teaspoon dried thyme
$1/4$ teaspoon dried tarragon
$1/8$ teaspoon ground red pepper
1   large apple, cut into matchsticks

1. In a large skillet, cook the bacon over medium-high heat for 5 minutes, stirring occasionally, or until crisp. With a slotted spoon, transfer the bacon to paper towels.

2. Add the onion to the skillet and cook over medium-high heat for 5 minutes, stirring occasionally, or until soft. Add the cabbage, water, vinegar, salt, thyme, tarragon, and ground red pepper. Bring to a boil. Reduce the heat and simmer, covered, for 10 minutes, stirring occasionally, or until the flavors are blended and the cabbage is tender-crisp.

3. Add the apple and bacon and cook, uncovered, for 5 minutes, or until the liquid has evaporated and the apple is softened.

Per serving: 104 calories ▶ 3 g protein ▶ 15 g carbohydrates ▶ 4 g fat ▶ 1 g saturated fat ▶ 4 g fiber ▶ 394 mg sodium

BLT SALAD

A salad version of America's favorite sandwich. Add slices of grilled chicken or steak for a quick and easy main dish.

Prep time: 15 minutes
Total time: 20 minutes
Makes 4 servings

¼ cup red wine vinaigrette
1 tablespoon mayonnaise
1 medium head romaine lettuce, torn
4 small tomatoes, chopped
1 cup fresh basil leaves, torn
6 slices crumbled crisp-cooked turkey bacon
2 ounces Parmesan cheese, thinly shaved with a vegetable peeler

1. In a large bowl, whisk together the vinaigrette and mayonnaise until blended. Add the lettuce, tomatoes, and basil. Toss to coat well.

2. Divide the salad among 4 plates. Sprinkle with the bacon and top with the Parmesan shavings.

Per serving: 184 calories ▸ 14 g protein ▸ 11 g carbohydrates ▸ 11 g fat ▸ 2 g saturated fat ▸ 5 g fiber ▸ 288 mg sodium

PEAR AND CRESS SALAD

Asian pears, often called apple pears, are crisp, juicy, and slightly sweet. They are round in shape with speckled bronze skin. If you can't find Asian pears, Bosc or Anjou pears will work just as well.

Prep time: 15 minutes
Total time: 20 minutes
Makes 4 servings

2   tablespoons orange juice
2   tablespoons canola oil
2   tablespoons apple cider vinegar
2   teaspoons reduced-sodium soy sauce
¼   teaspoon ground ginger
¼   teaspoon salt
2   bunches watercress, tough stems trimmed
1   small bulb fennel, thinly sliced
1   Asian pear, cut into matchsticks
3   tablespoons sliced almonds, toasted

1. In a large bowl, whisk together the orange juice, oil, vinegar, soy sauce, ginger, and salt. Add the watercress, fennel, and pear. Toss to coat well.

2. Divide the watercress mixture among 4 plates. Top with the almonds.

Per serving: 113 calories ▶ 3 g protein ▶ 6 g carbohydrates ▶ 9 g fat ▶ 0.5 g saturated fat ▶ 2 g fiber ▶ 258 mg sodium

GRAPEFRUIT, PECAN, AND MONTEREY JACK SALAD

For more crunch and fiber, add 1 chopped Granny Smith apple.

Prep time: 20 minutes
Total time: 35 minutes
Makes 4 servings

---

2 ruby red grapefruits
2 tablespoons olive oil
2 teaspoons honey mustard
½ teaspoon salt
⅛ teaspoon ground black pepper
1 container (5 ounces) mixed baby greens
1 red bell pepper, cut into thin strips
⅓ cup coarsely shredded Monterey Jack cheese
⅓ cup pecans, toasted and chopped

1. With a small knife, cut away the peel and white pith from each grapefruit. Working over a small bowl, cut the flesh into segments, cutting them out of their membranes into the bowl. Squeeze the juice from the membranes. With a slotted spoon, transfer the grapefruit segments to a large bowl, leaving the juices behind. Whisk the oil, honey mustard, salt, and pepper into the juice.

2. Add the greens and bell pepper to the grapefruit sections; drizzle with the juice mixture, tossing gently to coat well.

3. Divide the salad among 4 plates. Top with the cheese and pecans.

Per serving: 176 calories ▶ 4 g protein ▶ 12 g carbohydrates ▶ 14 g fat ▶ 3 g saturated fat ▶ 3 g fiber ▶ 290 mg sodium

CAULIFLOWER AND PICKLE SALAD

Dill pickles make a nice addition to this salad and are a sugar-blocking star. Add pepperoncini or a few oil-cured black olives to the salad if you like.

Prep time: 20 minutes
Total time: 30 minutes + marinating time
Makes 4 servings

---

1   small head cauliflower, broken into large florets, cut into ½"-thick slices
3   tablespoons olive oil
3   tablespoons white wine vinegar
1   clove garlic, minced
¼   teaspoon salt
¼   teaspoon ground black pepper
½   red bell pepper, chopped
2   large dill pickle spears, chopped
1   rib celery, chopped

1. Bring a medium saucepan of water to a boil over high heat. Cook the cauliflower for 2 minutes, or until tender-crisp. Drain and rinse under cold water; drain well.

2. In a large bowl, whisk together the oil, vinegar, garlic, salt, and black pepper until blended. Add the cauliflower, bell pepper, pickles, and celery. Toss to coat well. Let stand 30 minutes before serving. Or cover and refrigerate for up to 2 days.

Per serving: 125 calories ▶ 3 g protein ▶ 7 g carbohydrates ▶ 11 g fat ▶ 1.5 g saturated fat ▶ 3 g fiber ▶ 354 mg sodium

RADISH, CUCUMBER, AND BLUE CHEESE SALAD

To make ahead, place the lettuce, radishes, and cucumber, without the dressing, in a large bowl covered with a damp paper towel and plastic wrap. Toss with the dressing right before serving.

Prep time: 15 minutes
Total time: 20 minutes
Makes 4 servings

- 2 tablespoons sour cream
- 2 tablespoons apple cider vinegar
- 1 tablespoon mayonnaise
- ⅛ teaspoon stevia
- ¼ teaspoon salt
- 1 head romaine lettuce, halved lengthwise and thickly sliced crosswise
- 6 radishes, thinly sliced
- ½ hothouse (seedless) cucumber, halved lengthwise and cut crosswise into half-moons
- ½ cup crumbled blue cheese

1. In a large bowl, whisk together the sour cream, vinegar, mayonnaise, stevia, and salt.

2. Add the lettuce, radishes, and cucumber. Toss to coat well. Sprinkle with the blue cheese.

Per serving: 125 calories ▶ 5 g protein ▶ 4 g carbohydrates ▶ 10 g fat ▶ 4 g saturated fat ▶ 3 g fiber ▶ 413 mg sodium

ORANGE AND RADISH SALAD

Allowing the onion to macerate in a mixture of vinegar and water softens and mellows its flavor slightly.

Prep time: 15 minutes
Total time: 35 minutes
Makes 4 servings

- ¼ cup water
- ¼ cup + 2 tablespoons red wine vinegar
- ½ medium red onion, thinly sliced
- 2 navel oranges
- 2 tablespoons olive oil
- ¼ teaspoon salt
- 6 radishes, thinly sliced
- ¾ cup loosely packed fresh mint leaves
- 3 cups mixed baby greens

1. In a medium bowl, combine the water and ¼ cup of the vinegar. Add the onion and let stand 15 minutes, or until softened. Drain.

2. Meanwhile, with a small knife, cut away the peel and white pith from each orange. Cut the oranges crosswise into rounds, then cut the rounds in half.

3. In a large bowl, whisk together the oil, salt, and remaining 2 tablespoons vinegar. Add the orange slices, radishes, and mint. Toss to coat well.

4. Divide the greens among 4 plates. Top with the orange mixture and sprinkle with the onion.

Per serving: 116 calories ▶ 2 g protein ▶ 12 g carbohydrates ▶ 7 g fat ▶ 1 g saturated fat ▶ 3 g fiber ▶ 163 mg sodium

LENTIL, ZUCCHINI, AND CHICORY SALAD

Lentils are very nutritious: High in protein and fiber, they can help lower cholesterol and stabilize blood sugar. If you prefer to use dried lentils instead of canned, simmer ½ cup dried lentils in 2 cups water for about 20 minutes, or until tender.

Prep time: 15 minutes
Total time: 20 minutes
Makes 4 servings

1   can (15 ounces) lentils, rinsed and drained
1   zucchini, cut into ½" chunks
1   carrot, cut into ½" cubes
1   tomato, chopped
⅓   cup Italian salad dressing
1   teaspoon grated lemon peel
4   cups coarsely chopped chicory or curly endive

1. In a large bowl, combine the lentils, zucchini, carrot, and tomato. Add the dressing and lemon peel, tossing to coat well.

2. Divide the chicory among 4 plates and top with the lentil mixture.

Per serving: 107 calories ▸ 5 g protein ▸ 14 g carbohydrates ▸ 4 g fat ▸ 0.5 g saturated fat ▸ 6 g fiber ▸ 315 mg sodium

CREAMY BROCCOLI SALAD

Add ¼ cup toasted walnuts and a few seedless red grapes if you like.

Prep time: 15 minutes
Total time: 20 minutes
Makes 6 servings

6 cups broccoli florets, coarsely chopped
¼ cup apple cider vinegar
3 tablespoons mayonnaise
2 tablespoons 2% plain Greek yogurt
1 tablespoon chopped fresh dill
1 teaspoon grated lemon peel
½ teaspoon hot-pepper sauce
1 Granny Smith apple, chopped
½ small red onion, thinly sliced

1. In a large microwaveable bowl, combine the broccoli and ¼ cup water. Cover and microwave on high power for 2 minutes, or until tender-crisp. Drain and rinse under cold water; drain well.

2. Meanwhile, in a large bowl, whisk together the vinegar, mayonnaise, yogurt, dill, lemon peel, and hot sauce until blended.

3. Add the broccoli, apple, and onion. Toss to coat well.

Per serving: 110 calories ▸ 3 g protein ▸ 11 g carbohydrates ▸ 7 g fat ▸ 1 g saturated fat ▸ 4 g fiber ▸ 83 mg sodium

GREEN GODDESS SALAD

The dressing may be used to serve over grilled chicken or fish.

Prep time: 15 minutes
Total time: 20 minutes
Makes 4 servings

3   tablespoons mayonnaise
2   tablespoons reduced-fat sour cream
1   tablespoon tarragon vinegar
1   tablespoon chopped fresh dill
1   scallion, finely chopped
    Grated peel of 1 lemon
¼   teaspoon salt
1   container (5 ounces) mixed baby greens
1   head radicchio, thinly sliced
½   small cucumber, thinly sliced

In a large bowl, whisk together the mayonnaise, sour cream, vinegar, dill, scallion, lemon peel, and salt. Add the greens, radicchio, and cucumber. Toss to coat well.

Per serving: 101 calories ▶ 2 g protein ▶ 3 g carbohydrates ▶ 9 g fat ▶ 1.5 g saturated fat ▶ 2 g fiber ▶ 222 mg sodium

SPICY CUCUMBER SALAD

If you like, use whole leaves of Bibb or Boston lettuce and spoon the cucumber mixture into the lettuce cups.

Prep time: 15 minutes
Total time: 25 minutes + chilling time
Makes 4 servings

2	tablespoons white wine vinegar
1	tablespoon reduced-sodium soy sauce
1	tablespoon toasted sesame oil
¼	teaspoon red-pepper flakes
⅛	teaspoon salt
2	cucumbers, peeled and cut into 1" chunks
4	leaves romaine lettuce, thinly sliced
1	scallion, thinly sliced

1. In a large bowl, whisk together the vinegar, soy sauce, sesame oil, red-pepper flakes, and salt. Add the cucumbers and toss to coat well. Cover and refrigerate 30 minutes to allow the flavors to blend.

2. Divide the lettuce among 4 plates. Top with the cucumber mixture and scallion.

Per serving: 47 calories ▶ 1 g protein ▶ 3 g carbohydrates ▶ 4 g fat ▶ 0.5 g saturated fat ▶ 1 g fiber ▶ 209 mg sodium

FENNEL AND APPLE SALAD

If you're not fond of fennel, you can use celery instead.
You will need about 3 large ribs for this recipe.

Prep time: 10 minutes
Total time: 20 minutes
Makes 4 servings

1   navel orange
2   tablespoons apple cider vinegar
2   tablespoons olive oil
¼   teaspoon salt
⅛   teaspoon ground black pepper
1   small bulb fennel, thinly sliced
1   Granny Smith apple, thinly sliced

1. Grate the peel from the orange into a small bowl. With a small knife, cut away the peel and white pith. Cut the flesh into segments, cutting them out of the membranes into the bowl. Squeeze the juice from the membranes. With a slotted spoon, transfer the orange segments to a large bowl, leaving the juices behind. Whisk the vinegar, oil, salt, and pepper into the juice.

2. Add the fennel and apple to the orange sections. Drizzle with the juice mixture and toss to coat well.

Per serving: 116 calories ▶ 1 g protein ▶ 14 g carbohydrates ▶ 7 g fat ▶ 1 g saturated fat ▶ 3 g fiber ▶ 177 mg sodium

SPINACH SALAD WITH STRAWBERRIES

Try a variation of this salad by using baby salad greens instead of spinach and 2 cups blackberries instead of the strawberries.

Prep time: 10 minutes
Total time: 15 minutes
Makes 4 servings

---

1   container (5 ounces) baby spinach
½   pound strawberries, sliced
1   cup fresh mint leaves, torn
⅓   cup almonds, toasted and coarsely chopped
1   tablespoon apple cider vinegar
¼   cup ranch salad dressing

1. In a large bowl, combine the spinach, strawberries, mint, almonds, and vinegar. Toss to coat well.

2. Divide the spinach mixture among 4 plates. Drizzle with the dressing.

Per serving: 180 calories ▶ 4 g protein ▶ 13 g carbohydrates ▶ 14 g fat ▶ 1.5 g saturated fat ▶ 5 g fiber ▶ 183 mg sodium

TOMATOES WITH OLIVES AND LEMON

If you like, add ¼ cup roasted red bell pepper strips and a few tablespoons of chopped fresh basil to the salad.

Prep time: 15 minutes
Total time: 15 minutes
Makes 4 servings

- 2 tablespoons red wine vinegar
- 2 tablespoons extra-virgin olive oil
- 1 teaspoon grated lemon peel
- ¼ teaspoon salt
- ⅛ teaspoon ground black pepper
- 3 cups mixed baby greens
- 3 tomatoes, cut into wedges
- ¼ cup pitted kalamata olives, sliced
- ½ ounce Parmesan cheese, thinly shaved with a vegetable peeler

1. In a small bowl, whisk together the vinegar, oil, lemon peel, salt, and pepper.

2. Divide the greens, tomatoes, and olives among 4 plates. Drizzle with the dressing and top with the Parmesan shavings.

Per serving: 117 calories ▸ 3 g protein ▸ 6 g carbohydrates ▸ 10 g fat ▸ 1.5 g saturated fat ▸ 2 g fiber ▸ 373 mg sodium

SNAP PEA SALAD WITH CARROT-GINGER DRESSING

The carrot gives the dressing a hint of sweetness without any added sugar.

Prep time: 20 minutes
Total time: 30 minutes
Makes 4 servings

½   pound sugar snap peas, strings removed
1   small carrot, sliced
2   tablespoons chopped fresh ginger
1   scallion, thinly sliced
2   tablespoons rice wine vinegar
1   tablespoon canola oil
1   tablespoon water
2   teaspoons toasted sesame oil
¼   teaspoon salt
1   head Boston lettuce, torn into bite-size pieces
1   red bell pepper, chopped

1. Bring a small saucepan of water to a boil over high heat. Cook the sugar snaps for 4 minutes, or until tender-crisp. Drain and rinse under cold water; drain well.

2. Meanwhile, in a blender, combine the carrot, ginger, scallion, vinegar, canola oil, water, sesame oil, and salt. Process until smooth.

3. In a large bowl, combine the lettuce, bell pepper, and sugar snaps. Add the dressing and toss to coat well.

Per serving: 97 calories ► 2 g protein ► 9 g carbohydrates ► 6 g fat ► 0.5 g saturated fat ► 3 g fiber ► 165 mg sodium

TOMATO-EDAMAME SALAD

Edamame and black beans are high in protein and favorable for sugar blocking.

Prep time: 15 minutes
Total time: 25 minutes
Makes 4 servings

1   cup frozen shelled edamame
3   tablespoons olive oil
2   tablespoons apple cider vinegar
1   teaspoon grated lime peel
1/4   teaspoon chipotle chile powder
1/4   teaspoon salt
1   cup grape tomatoes, halved
3/4   cup canned black beans, rinsed and drained
1   carrot, shredded
2   scallions, thinly sliced

1. Bring a small saucepan of water to a boil over high heat. Cook the edamame for 4 minutes, or until tender. Drain and rinse under cold water; drain well.

2. In a large bowl, whisk together the oil, vinegar, lime peel, chipotle powder, and salt. Add the tomatoes, beans, carrot, scallions, and edamame. Toss to coat well.

Per serving: 180 calories ▶ 7 g protein ▶ 12 g carbohydrates ▶ 13 g fat ▶ 1.5 g saturated fat ▶ 5 g fiber ▶ 196 mg sodium

ASPARAGUS AND RED ONION SALAD

Broccoli, cauliflower, or green beans may be used in place of the asparagus.

Prep time: 15 minutes
Total time: 25 minutes
Makes 4 servings

- 1 red onion, cut into ½"-thick slices
- 1 bunch asparagus, cut into 2" pieces
- 2 tablespoons apple cider vinegar
- 2 tablespoons olive oil
- 1 teaspoon Dijon mustard
- 1 clove garlic, minced
- ¼ teaspoon smoked paprika
- ¼ teaspoon salt

1. Coat a nonstick ridged grill pan with cooking spray and set over medium heat. Cook the onion for 8 minutes, turning once, or until tender and lightly charred. Transfer to a cutting board to cool slightly. Then cut the slices in half.

2. Bring a medium saucepan of water to a boil over high heat. Cook the asparagus for 2 minutes, or until tender-crisp. Drain and rinse under cold water; drain well.

3. Meanwhile, in a large bowl, whisk together the vinegar, oil, mustard, garlic, paprika, and salt.

4. Add the asparagus and onion to the dressing, tossing to coat well.

Per serving: 88 calories ▶ 2 g protein ▶ 6 g carbohydrates ▶ 7 g fat ▶ 1 g saturated fat ▶ 2 g fiber ▶ 178 mg sodium

COCONUT WAFFLES WITH
TWO-BERRY SYRUP

(*page 72*)

GARDEN WRAP

(*page 86*)

DELUXE HAM PANINI
(page 92)

OPEN-FACED STEAK
SANDWICHES
(page 98)

SOBA NOODLE
SALAD

(*page 113*)

SHRIMP CRACKERS WITH
WASABI CREAM CHEESE

(page 119)

WALNUT AND BLUE CHEESE BALL

(page 125)

GRAPEFRUIT, PECAN, AND MONTEREY JACK SALAD

(page 139)

SLOW-COOKED POT ROAST
(*page 162*)

CHUNKY GARLIC MASHED POTATOES
(*page 210*)

SMOKY ROAST PORK
AND PLUMS
(*page 167*)

BULGUR PILAF
WITH WILD RICE
(*page 208*)

TOMATO-BASIL CHICKEN
(*page 181*)

SHRIMP SCAMPI PASTA

(*page 187*)

ROAST PEACHES WITH
STREUSEL TOPPING

(*page 234*)

FRESH FRUIT TART

(page 236)

CHOCOLATE POTS DE CRÈME

(*page 243*)

PEANUT BUTTER
CHOCOLATE CHIP COOKIES
(page 250)

ALMOND BUTTER
SHORTBREAD COOKIES
(page 251)

ICEBERG WEDGES WITH BUTTERMILK DRESSING

Crunchy iceberg lettuce is classic, but you can use 2 hearts of romaine, each cut lengthwise in half, if you prefer.

Prep time: 15 minutes
Total time: 25 minutes
Makes 4 servings

½   cup ranch dressing
⅓   cup crumbled blue cheese
2   teaspoons apple cider vinegar
1   head iceberg lettuce, cut into 4 wedges
1   large tomato, chopped
4   slices crumbled crisp-cooked bacon
1   tablespoon chopped fresh chives

1. In a small bowl, combine the ranch dressing, blue cheese, and vinegar until well mixed.

2. Divide the lettuce wedges among 4 plates. Drizzle each with the dressing and top with the tomato, bacon, and chives.

Per serving: 377 calories ▸ 8 g protein ▸ 6 g carbohydrates ▸ 36 g fat ▸ 10 g saturated fat ▸ 2 g fiber ▸ 728 mg sodium

ARUGULA AND GRAPEFRUIT SALAD

Olive oil, avocado, and pecans make this salad a sugar-blocking star.

Prep time: 15 minutes
Total time: 20 minutes
Makes 4 servings

- 2 tablespoons olive oil
- 2 tablespoons rice wine vinegar
- ¼ teaspoon salt
- 6 cups baby arugula
- 1 pink grapefruit, peeled and cut into segments
- 1 Hass avocado, pitted, peeled, and cubed
- ⅓ cup pecans, toasted and coarsely chopped

In a large bowl, whisk together the oil, vinegar, and salt. Add the arugula, grapefruit segments, avocado, and pecans. Toss gently to combine well.

Per serving: 231 calories ▸ 3 g protein ▸ 13 g carbohydrates ▸ 21 g fat ▸ 2.5 g saturated fat ▸ 6 g fiber ▸ 157 mg sodium

CELERY AND APPLE SALAD

If you're pressed for time, use 1 bag (16 ounces) coleslaw mix instead of the cabbage.

Prep time: 15 minutes
Total time: 20 minutes
Makes 4 servings

3 tablespoons red wine vinegar
2 tablespoons canola oil
1 tablespoon toasted sesame oil
4 teaspoons sweet garlic-chili sauce
½ teaspoon salt
1 small head napa cabbage, shredded
1 apple, cut into matchsticks
2 ribs celery, thinly sliced
3 scallions, chopped
⅓ cup slivered almonds, toasted

In a large bowl, whisk together the vinegar, canola oil, sesame oil, garlic-chili sauce, and salt until blended. Add the cabbage, apple, celery, and scallions. Toss to coat well. Sprinkle with the almonds.

Per serving: 192 calories ▶ 3 g protein ▶ 12 g carbohydrates ▶ 15 g fat ▶ 1.5 g saturated fat ▶ 3 g fiber ▶ 358 mg sodium

PICKLED VEGETABLE SALAD

The pickled vegetables will keep in an airtight container in the refrigerator for up to 3 days.

Prep time: 15 minutes
Total time: 25 minutes +
cooling and chilling time
Makes 6 servings

3   carrots, cut on the diagonal into ½"-thick slices
1   cup distilled white vinegar
½   cup water
2   garlic cloves, crushed with the flat side of a knife
1   teaspoon salt-free spicy seasoning blend
¼   teaspoon salt
8   radishes, quartered lengthwise
1   small cucumber, cut into ¾" chunks
1   cup canned kidney beans, rinsed and drained
1   packet stevia

1. In a small saucepan, combine the carrots, vinegar, water, garlic, seasoning blend, and salt and bring to a boil. Cook for 5 minutes to blend the flavors.

2. Transfer the carrot mixture to a large bowl. Add the radishes, cucumber, beans, and stevia. Let the mixture cool to room temperature, about 1 hour. Refrigerate, covered, for at least 3 hours or overnight.

Per serving: 57 calories ▶ 3 g protein ▶ 11 g carbohydrates ▶ 0 g fat ▶ 0 g saturated fat ▶ 3 g fiber ▶ 412 mg sodium

ASIAN CABBAGE SLAW

Napa cabbage is also called Chinese cabbage. It has a milder flavor and more delicate texture than green cabbage. Look for heads that are tightly packed.

Prep time: 20 minutes
Total time: 25 minutes
Makes 4 servings

- 2   tablespoons canola oil
- 2   tablespoons rice wine vinegar
- 2   tablespoons reduced-sodium soy sauce
- 2   teaspoons toasted sesame oil
- 1   teaspoon grated fresh ginger
- ½   head napa cabbage, shredded
- 1   cup sliced cremini mushrooms
- 2   ribs celery, thinly sliced
- 1   carrot, grated
- 2   scallions, thinly sliced
- ¼   cup unsalted peanuts, coarsely chopped

In a large bowl, whisk together the oil, vinegar, soy sauce, sesame oil, and ginger until blended. Add the cabbage, mushrooms, celery, carrot, scallions, and peanuts. Toss to coat well.

Per serving: 172 calories ▸ 4 g protein ▸ 9 g carbohydrates ▸ 14 g fat ▸ 1.5 g saturated fat ▸ 3 g fiber ▸ 308 mg sodium

MAIN DISHES

HERB-CRUSTED STEAK WITH POTATO FRIES

A generous amount of protein, along with the fat from the olive oil and Parmesan cheese, helps to block the starch from the potatoes.

Prep time: 15 minutes
Total time: 1 hour 10 minutes + marinating time
Makes 4 servings

- 3 tablespoons olive oil, divided
- 1 tablespoon balsamic vinegar
- 2 teaspoons Dijon mustard
- 2 teaspoons chopped fresh rosemary
- 1 clove garlic, minced
- ½ teaspoon dried thyme
- ½ teaspoon salt, divided
- ½ teaspoon ground black pepper, divided
- 1¼ pounds sirloin steak
- 2 medium (5 ounces each) baking potatoes, each cut lengthwise into 8 wedges
- ¼ cup grated Parmesan cheese

1. Preheat the oven to 425°F.

2. In a large resealable plastic food storage bag, combine 1 tablespoon of the oil, the vinegar, mustard, rosemary, garlic, thyme, ¼ teaspoon of the salt, and ¼ teaspoon of the pepper. Add the steak. Squeeze out the air and seal the bag; turn to coat the steak. Refrigerate for 20 minutes, turning the bag occasionally.

3. Coat a rimmed baking sheet with cooking spray. On the baking sheet, toss the potatoes with the remaining 2 tablespoons oil, remaining ¼ teaspoon salt, and remaining ¼ teaspoon pepper. Spread the potatoes evenly in the pan and roast for 20 minutes. Turn the potatoes and roast for 15 minutes, or until browned and crisp. Evenly sprinkle with the cheese and bake for 3 minutes, or until the cheese just begins to melt.

4. Meanwhile, coat a nonstick ridged grill pan with cooking spray and heat over medium-high heat. Cook the steak for 8 minutes, turning once, or until a thermometer inserted in the center registers 145°F for medium-rare. Transfer to a cutting board and let stand for 10 minutes before slicing across the grain. Serve the steak with the potatoes.

Per serving: 366 calories ▶ 35 g protein ▶ 14 g carbohydrates ▶ 19 g fat ▶ 5 g saturated fat ▶ 2 g fiber ▶ 513 mg sodium

GRILLED STEAK AND PEACH SALAD

When buying stone fruits for grilling, look for fruits that are firm and have good color. Avoid fruits that are soft or bruised, as they will turn mushy when cooked.

Prep time: 20 minutes
Total time: 40 minutes
Makes 4 servings

1   tablespoon chia seeds
3   tablespoons red wine vinegar
2   tablespoons olive oil
1   teaspoon salt, divided
2   large ripe peaches, halved and pitted
1   pound sirloin steak, trimmed of all visible fat
2   teaspoons salt-free seasoning
1   package (8 ounces) mixed baby greens
1   cup grape or cherry tomatoes, halved
2   ribs celery, thinly sliced
¼   cup chopped fresh mint

1. In a large bowl, combine the chia seeds and ⅓ cup water. Let stand for 5 minutes to thicken slightly. Stir in the vinegar, oil, and ½ teaspoon of the salt until blended. Set the dressing aside.

2. Coat a grill rack or nonstick grill pan with cooking spray and preheat to medium.

3. Coat the cut surfaces of the peaches with cooking spray. Sprinkle the steak with the seasoning and the remaining ½ teaspoon salt. Place the steak and peaches, cut sides down, on the grill or grill pan. Grill the peaches for 6 minutes, or until soft. Grill the steak for 8 minutes, turning once, or until a thermometer inserted in the center registers 145°F for medium-rare. Let stand for 5 minutes before thinly slicing.

4. Slice the peaches into wedges. Add the greens, tomatoes, celery, and mint to the bowl of dressing and toss to coat well.

5. Divide the salad among 4 plates and top with the sliced steak and peaches.

Per serving: 375 calories ▶ 36 g protein ▶ 14 g carbohydrates ▶ 20 g fat ▶ 5.5 g saturated fat ▶ 5 g fiber ▶ 686 mg sodium

SLOW-COOKED POT ROAST

No worries if there are leftovers: Heat the shredded beef with salsa and serve with warm low-carb tortillas.

Prep time: 15 minutes
Total time: 5 hours 15 minutes
Makes 8 servings

1   can (14.5 ounces) stewed tomatoes
2   tablespoons tomato paste
1   teaspoon dried thyme
3½   pounds boneless beef chuck roast, trimmed of all visible fat
1   large Vidalia onion, thinly sliced
2   large carrots, sliced
½   ounce dried porcini mushrooms

1. In a 5- to 6-quart slow cooker, mix together the tomatoes, tomato paste, and thyme. Place the beef on top of the sauce and spoon some sauce over the beef. Scatter the onion, carrots, and dried mushrooms around the beef.

2. Cover and cook for 5 to 6 hours on high or 8 to 10 hours on low, or until the beef and vegetables are fork-tender.

3. Transfer the beef to a cutting board and let stand 10 minutes before slicing across the grain. Serve with the vegetables and sauce.

Per serving: 334 calories ▸ 44 g protein ▸ 12 g carbohydrates ▸ 11 g fat ▸ 4 g saturated fat ▸ 3 g fiber ▸ 306 mg sodium

ITALIAN MEAT LOAF

Serve with broccoli rabe sautéed in garlic and olive oil to round out the meal.

Prep time: 15 minutes

Total time: 1 hour 35 minutes

Makes 6 servings

2	teaspoons olive oil
1/2	package (10 ounces) mushrooms, coarsely chopped
1	small onion, finely chopped
2	cloves garlic, minced
1 1/4	pounds lean ground beef
1	cup no-sugar-added tomato sauce, divided
3/4	cup quick-cooking oats
1/3	cup grated Romano cheese
1	egg, lightly beaten
2	teaspoons Italian seasoning
1/2	teaspoon salt

1. Preheat the oven to 350°F. Line a rimmed baking sheet with foil. Coat the foil lightly with cooking spray.

2. Warm the oil in a large nonstick skillet over medium-high heat. Cook the mushrooms, onion, and garlic for 6 minutes, stirring occasionally, or until softened and most of the liquid has evaporated. Transfer to a large bowl and let cool 5 minutes.

3. Add the beef, 1/2 cup of the tomato sauce, the oats, cheese, egg, Italian seasoning, and salt to the bowl. Gently mix to combine. Transfer the mixture to the baking sheet and form into an 8" × 5" loaf. Spread the remaining 1/2 cup tomato sauce over the top of the loaf. Bake for 1 hour 10 minutes, or until a thermometer inserted in the center registers 160°F and the meat is no longer pink.

Per serving: 241 calories ▶ 26 g protein ▶ 11 g carbohydrates ▶ 11 g fat ▶ 3 g saturated fat ▶ 3 g fiber ▶ 473 mg sodium

BEEF AND ORANGE STIR-FRY

Serve this stir-fry over warmed shirataki noodles or cooked brown rice. If you like, substitute your favorite fresh vegetables for the frozen bell pepper medley.

Prep time: 15 minutes
Total time: 25 minutes
Makes 4 servings

2   navel oranges
3   teaspoons vegetable oil, divided
¾   pound beef sirloin, cut across the grain into ¼"-thick slices
1   package (12 ounces) frozen bell pepper and onion strips, thawed
1   package (8 ounces) sugar snap peas, strings removed
3   tablespoons stir-fry sauce
1   tablespoon chopped fresh ginger
¼   teaspoon red-pepper flakes

1. Grate the peel from 1 orange into a medium bowl. With a small knife, cut away the peel and white pith from both oranges. Cut the flesh into segments, cutting them out of their membranes. Slice the segments in half and add to the bowl.

2. Heat 1 teaspoon of the oil in a large nonstick skillet or wok over medium-high heat. Cook the beef for 3 minutes, stirring, or until the beef is browned. Transfer to a plate.

3. Add the remaining 2 teaspoons oil to the skillet and heat over medium-high heat. Cook the bell pepper mixture for 2 minutes, or until softened. Add the sugar snaps, stir-fry sauce, ginger, and red-pepper flakes. Cook for 2 minutes, stirring occasionally, or until the sugar snaps are tender-crisp. Return the beef to the skillet and cook for 2 minutes, or until heated through.

4. Divide the beef mixture among 4 plates and top with the orange mixture.

Per serving: 311 calories ► 20 g protein ► 21 g carbohydrates ► 16 g fat ► 5 g saturated fat ► 4 g fiber ► 165 mg sodium

CHEDDAR AND PICKLE BURGERS

Be sure to read labels when selecting thin sliced bread for sandwiches. The calories and carb grams can vary greatly from brand to brand—always opt for those with the least amount of both.

Prep time: 20 minutes
Total time: 30 minutes
Makes 4 servings

1   pound lean ground beef sirloin
3   ounces reduced-fat Cheddar cheese, cut into ¼" cubes
½   cup chopped dill pickles
¼   cup light mayonnaise, divided
2   tablespoons ketchup
2   teaspoons yellow mustard
4   slices very thinly sliced whole wheat bread
4   leaves green leaf lettuce
1   tomato, sliced

1. In a large bowl, mix together the beef, cheese, pickles, and 2 tablespoons of the mayonnaise. Form the mixture into 4 patties.

2. Coat a large nonstick skillet with cooking spray and heat over medium heat. Cook the patties for 10 minutes, turning once, or until a thermometer inserted in the center registers 160°F and the meat is no longer pink.

3. Meanwhile, in a small bowl, stir together the ketchup, mustard, and the remaining 2 tablespoons mayonnaise until blended.

4. Divide the bread among 4 plates. Evenly spread all the bread with the ketchup mixture. Top 4 slices with a burger, lettuce, and tomato. Top with the remaining bread.

Per serving: 346 calories ▸ 31 g protein ▸ 20 g carbohydrates ▸ 16 g fat ▸ 6 g saturated fat ▸ 3 g fiber ▸ 781 mg sodium

PORK FAJITAS

Planning ahead can save you time in the kitchen later. Slice the pork, onion, and bell peppers several hours or up to a day ahead, and store the meat and vegetables separately in resealable plastic food storage bags.

Prep time: 20 minutes
Total time: 35 minutes
Makes 6 servings

- ¼ cup sour cream
- 2 tablespoons chopped fresh cilantro
- 1 tablespoon red wine vinegar
- 1 pound pork tenderloin, sliced crosswise and cut into thin strips
- 2 teaspoons Mexican seasoning blend, divided
- 2 teaspoons olive oil, divided
- 2 bell peppers, thinly sliced
- 1 onion, thinly sliced
- 6 low-carb tortillas (7" diameter), warmed
- 2 tomatoes, chopped
- 1 avocado, cut into ½" pieces

1. In a small bowl, mix together the sour cream, cilantro, and vinegar.

2. Sprinkle both sides of the pork with 1½ teaspoons of the Mexican seasoning blend. Heat 1 teaspoon of the oil in a large nonstick skillet over medium-high heat. Cook the pork for 5 minutes, stirring, or until no longer pink. Transfer to a plate.

3. Warm the remaining 1 teaspoon oil in the same skillet over medium-high heat. Cook the bell peppers, onion, and remaining ½ teaspoon Mexican seasoning blend for 4 minutes, stirring occasionally, or until tender-crisp. Return the pork to the skillet and cook for 2 minutes, or until heated through.

4. Divide the pork mixture among the tortillas. Top with the tomatoes, avocado, and sour cream mixture.

....

Per serving: 238 calories ▸ 23 g protein ▸ 18 g carbohydrates ▸ 12 g fat ▸ 2 g saturated fat ▸ 11 g fiber ▸ 120 mg sodium

SMOKY ROAST PORK AND PLUMS

This is equally delicious with boneless pork tenderloin. You can add the plums right in with the pork and roast them together for about 20 minutes.

Prep time: 10 minutes
Total time: 1 hour 5 minutes
Makes 6 servings

2 teaspoons smoked paprika
1 teaspoon garlic salt
¾ teaspoon ground cumin
½ teaspoon ground cinnamon
1 boneless center-cut pork loin (about 2 pounds)
4 large plums, cut into wedges
2 tablespoons apricot fruit spread

1. Preheat the oven to 400°F. Line a small shallow roasting pan with foil. Coat the foil with cooking spray.

2. In a cup, mix together the smoked paprika, salt, cumin, and cinnamon. Sprinkle half of the paprika mixture all over the pork. Place the pork in the pan and roast for 30 minutes.

3. In a medium bowl, toss the plums with the fruit spread and remaining paprika mixture until well coated. Scatter evenly around the pork. Roast for 25 minutes, or until a thermometer inserted in the center of the pork registers 145°F and the plums are fork-tender. Let the pork stand 5 minutes before slicing. Serve with the plums.

Per serving: 262 calories ▸ 33 g protein ▸ 8 g carbohydrates ▸ 10 g fat ▸ 3.5 g saturated fat ▸ 1 g fiber ▸ 230 mg sodium

SKILLET PORK WITH SWEET POTATO AND APPLE

This savory meal must follow a sugar-blocking first course. Start the meal with a glass of wine along with the Hot and Sour Slaw (page 136), Green Goddess Salad (page 145), or the Asparagus and Red Onion Salad (page 152).

Prep time: 15 minutes
Total time: 1 hour 25 minutes
Makes 4 servings

---

2   tablespoons olive oil
1½ pounds boneless pork shoulder, cut into 1" pieces
½   cup low-sodium chicken broth
¼   cup apple cider vinegar
½   teaspoon five-spice powder
½   teaspoon dried thyme
1   teaspoon salt
2   apples, peeled and cubed
4   carrots, sliced
1   sweet potato, cubed
1   package (16 ounces) frozen pearl onions, thawed
2   teaspoons cornstarch
2   tablespoons cold water

1. Warm the oil in a Dutch oven over medium-high heat. Cook the pork for 5 minutes, turning, or until browned.

2. Add the broth, vinegar, five-spice powder, thyme, and salt. Bring to a boil. Reduce the heat to low, cover, and simmer for 1 hour.

3. Add the apples, carrots, sweet potato, and pearl onions to the Dutch oven and bring to a boil. Reduce the heat and simmer for 15 minutes, stirring occasionally, or until the meat, apples, and vegetables are tender.

4. In a cup, whisk together the cornstarch and water until blended. Stir the cornstarch mixture into the simmering stew and cook for 1 minute, stirring, or until the stew just begins to thicken.

Per serving: 449 calories ▶ 36 g protein ▶ 33 g carbohydrates ▶ 19 g fat ▶ 5 g saturated fat ▶ 5 g fiber ▶ 885 mg sodium

PORK WITH BOURBON CREAM SAUCE

Here is real comfort food. This flavorful dish is very low in carbs, making it perfect with one of the sweet potato recipes. Try Sweet Potato–Carrot Pancakes (page 214) or Butter-Roasted Sweet Potatoes (page 212).

Prep time: 10 minutes
Total time: 20 minutes
Makes 4 servings

1 tablespoon olive oil
4 boneless pork loin chops, trimmed
¼ teaspoon salt
2 tablespoons bourbon or apple cider
1 tablespoon spicy brown mustard
1 tablespoon steak sauce
¼ cup reduced-fat sour cream
3 scallions, chopped

1. Warm the oil in a large nonstick skillet over medium-high heat. Sprinkle the pork with the salt and cook for 6 minutes, turning once, or until browned.

2. In a small bowl, whisk together the bourbon, mustard, steak sauce, and 3 tablespoons water until blended. Stir the bourbon mixture into the skillet. Reduce the heat to medium, cover, and simmer for 1 minute, or until a thermometer inserted in the center of a chop registers 160°F, the juices run clear, and the sauce has thickened slightly. Transfer the pork to a platter.

3. Add the sour cream and scallions to the sauce in the skillet and cook for 1 minute, or until heated through. Spoon the sauce over the pork.

Per serving: 131 calories ► 8 g protein ► 2 g carbohydrates ► 8 g fat ► 2 g saturated fat ► 0 g fiber ► 265 mg sodium

PORK WITH PEPPERS, ONIONS, AND VINEGAR

If you prefer a little more heat, add 1 tablespoon sliced hot cherry peppers instead of the jalapeño.

Prep time: 10 minutes
Total time: 30 minutes
Makes 4 servings

3 tablespoons olive oil, divided
4 boneless pork loin chops (4 ounces each)
½ teaspoon dried oregano
½ teaspoon salt, divided
1 orange bell pepper, cut into 1" pieces
1 red bell pepper, cut into 1" pieces
1 onion, thinly sliced
4 cloves garlic, thinly sliced
¾ cup low-sodium chicken broth
1 tablespoon balsamic vinegar
1 tablespoon sliced pickled jalapeño peppers, chopped

1. Heat 1 tablespoon of the oil in a large nonstick skillet over medium-high heat. Sprinkle the pork with the oregano and ¼ teaspoon of the salt. Cook the pork for 6 minutes, turning once, or until browned. Transfer to a plate.

2. Warm the remaining 2 tablespoons of oil in the same skillet over medium-high heat. Cook the bell peppers, onion, and garlic for 5 minutes, stirring occasionally, or until the peppers begin to soften. Add the broth, vinegar, jalapeños, and remaining ¼ teaspoon salt. Simmer for 3 minutes, stirring occasionally. Return the pork (with any accumulated juices) to the skillet, and cook for 3 minutes, or until a thermometer inserted in the center of a chop registers 160°F and the juices run clear.

Per serving: 270 calories ▶ 27 g protein ▶ 7 g carbohydrates ▶ 15 g fat ▶ 3 g saturated fat ▶ 1 g fiber ▶ 387 mg sodium

ASIAN PORK BURGERS

For a quick and crunchy slaw, use 4 cups coleslaw mix from a 16-ounce package, instead of the lettuce.

Prep time: 20 minutes
Total time: 30 minutes
Makes 4 servings

1   pound lean ground pork
2   tablespoons reduced-sodium soy sauce
2   scallions, finely chopped
1   tablespoon hoisin sauce
1   teaspoon grated lime peel
1   tablespoon fresh lime juice
1   tablespoon rice wine vinegar
1   tablespoon toasted sesame oil
1   teaspoon grated fresh ginger
¼   teaspoon salt
1   head Boston lettuce, torn into bite-sized pieces
1   cucumber, peeled and thinly sliced
6   radishes, thinly sliced

1. In a large bowl, mix together the pork, soy sauce, scallions, and hoisin sauce. Form the mixture into 4 patties.

2. Coat a large nonstick grill pan with cooking spray and heat over medium heat. Grill the patties for 9 minutes, turning once, or until a thermometer inserted in the center registers 160°F.

3. Meanwhile, in a large bowl, whisk together the lime peel, lime juice, vinegar, sesame oil, ginger, and salt. Add the lettuce, cucumber, and radishes. Toss until well mixed. Serve with the burgers.

Per serving: 196 calories ▸ 25 g protein ▸ 6 g carbohydrates ▸ 8 g fat ▸ 2 g saturated fat ▸ 1 g fiber ▸ 559 mg sodium

ASIAN NOODLE BOWL
WITH SHREDDED CHICKEN

Shirataki noodles can be found in the refrigerated section of Asian markets, health food stores, and some supermarkets. If you can't find shirataki noodles, search for them online as there are many sources available.

Prep time: 20 minutes
Total time: 30 minutes
Makes 4 servings

---

2   packages (8 ounces each) shirataki noodles
2   cans (14.5 ounces each) low-sodium chicken broth
4   teaspoons reduced-sodium soy sauce
1   tablespoon chopped fresh ginger
1   teaspoon reduced-sodium fish sauce
1   pound bok choy, cut into ½"-wide slices
1   red bell pepper, cut into thin strips
1   carrot, shredded
¾   pound chicken tenders, cut into thin strips
1   teaspoon toasted sesame oil
5   scallions, thinly sliced
2   tablespoons coarsely chopped fresh cilantro
    Lime wedges, for serving

1. Prepare the noodles according to package directions. Drain well.

2. In a large saucepan, bring the broth, soy sauce, ginger, and fish sauce to a boil over high heat. Add the bok choy, bell pepper, and carrot and simmer for 5 minutes, stirring occasionally, or until the vegetables are tender-crisp. Add the chicken and cook for 4 minutes, or until the chicken is no longer pink. Remove from the heat and stir in the sesame oil and scallions.

3. Divide the noodles and soup among 4 bowls. Top with the cilantro and serve with the lime wedges.

....

Per serving: 175 calories ▶ 24 g protein ▶ 10 g carbohydrates ▶ 5 g fat ▶ 1 g saturated fat ▶ 2 g fiber ▶ 464 mg sodium

CHICKEN PROVENÇAL

This flavorful dish goes well with the Chunky Garlic Mashed Potatoes (page 210), Bulgur with Pistachios (page 209), or the Creamy Brown Rice with Mushrooms (page 204).

Prep time: 10 minutes
Total time: 1 hour
Makes 4 servings

½ teaspoon olive oil
1 pound boneless, skinless chicken thighs, trimmed and cut into 1½" pieces
1 cup canned no-salt-added diced tomatoes
1 cup canned no-salt-added tomato sauce
½ cup low-sodium chicken broth
½ cup dry white wine
¼ cup sliced pitted green olives
2 cloves garlic, minced
1½ teaspoons herbes de Provence
½ teaspoon salt
¼ teaspoon ground black pepper

1. Warm the oil in a large nonstick skillet over medium-high heat. Cook the chicken for 4 minutes, turning occasionally, or until browned.

2. Add the tomatoes, tomato sauce, broth, wine, olives, garlic, herbes de Provence, salt, and pepper. Bring to a boil over medium-high heat. Reduce the heat to low, cover, and simmer for 50 minutes, stirring occasionally, or until the flavors are blended and the mixture begins to thicken.

Per serving: 230 calories ▶ 24 g protein ▶ 10 g carbohydrates ▶ 7 g fat ▶ 1 g saturated fat ▶ 2 g fiber ▶ 790 mg sodium

TANDOORI ROAST CHICKEN

Use any leftovers to make an Indian-inspired chicken salad by combining the chicken with some chopped celery, scallions, plain Greek yogurt, ground cumin, curry powder, and a sprinkling of lime juice. Serve with low-carb tortillas.

Prep time: 10 minutes
Total time: 40 minutes + marinating time
Makes 4 servings

½ cup 2% plain Greek yogurt
½ small onion, chopped
1 tablespoon olive oil
1 tablespoon grated fresh ginger
1 tablespoon paprika
2 cloves garlic, halved
1 teaspoon ground cumin
¾ teaspoon ground coriander
½ teaspoon salt
¼ teaspoon ground red pepper
4 bone-in, skinless chicken breast halves
Lemon or lime wedges, for serving

1. In a blender, combine the yogurt, onion, oil, ginger, paprika, garlic, cumin, coriander, salt, and ground red pepper and blend until smooth. Scrape the marinade into a large resealable plastic food storage bag. Add the chicken. Squeeze out the air and seal the bag, turning to coat the chicken. Refrigerate for 1 hour, turning the bag occasionally.

2. Preheat the oven to 450°F. Line a rimmed baking sheet with foil. Coat the foil with cooking spray.

3. Place the chicken on the baking sheet. Spoon the remaining marinade over the top of the chicken. Bake for 30 minutes, or until a thermometer inserted in the thickest portion (without touching bone) registers 170°F and the juices run clear. Serve with lemon or lime wedges.

Per serving: 441 calories ▶ 50 g protein ▶ 3 g carbohydrates ▶ 24 g fat ▶ 7 g saturated fat ▶ 1 g fiber ▶ 357 mg sodium

CURRIED GRILLED CHICKEN LEGS

To broil the chicken legs, line a broiler-pan rack with foil. Coat the foil with cooking spray and preheat the broiler. Place the chicken on the broiler-pan rack and broil 8″ from the heat, following the cooking times in step 2.

Prep time: 15 minutes
Total time: 45 minutes + marinating time
Makes 4 servings

½ cup low-fat plain yogurt
1 small onion, grated
3 tablespoons fresh lemon juice
2 tablespoons grated fresh ginger
1 tablespoon canola oil
2 teaspoons ground cumin
1½ teaspoons salt
1 teaspoon curry powder
1 teaspoon garam masala
¼ teaspoon ground red pepper
4 whole chicken legs (drumstick and thigh), skinned

1. In a resealable plastic food storage bag, combine the yogurt, onion, lemon juice, ginger, oil, cumin, salt, curry powder, garam masala, and ground red pepper. Add the chicken. Squeeze out the air and seal the bag, turning to coat the chicken. Refrigerate, turning the bag occasionally, for at least 1 hour or up to overnight.

2. Coat a grill rack with cooking spray and preheat the grill to medium. Remove the chicken from the marinade. Discard the marinade. Grill the chicken for 25 to 30 minutes, turning occasionally, or until a thermometer inserted in the thickest portion registers 170°F and the juices run clear.

Per serving: 302 calories ▶ 46 g protein ▶ 3 g carbohydrates ▶ 11 g fat ▶ 2.5 g saturated fat ▶ 0 g fiber ▶ 638 mg sodium

CHICKEN PAPRIKASH

A simple way to crush caraway seeds is to gather them in a small pile on a cutting board and coat them lightly with cooking spray. With a large knife, crush the seeds with a rocking, back-and-forth motion. If using a spice grinder, pulse several times until the seeds are finely crushed.

Prep time: 15 minutes
Total time: 45 minutes
Makes 4 servings

1   tablespoon canola oil
1   pound boneless, skinless chicken breasts, cut into thin strips
1   large onion, thinly sliced
2   large bell peppers, thinly sliced
½   cup dry white wine
1   tablespoon paprika
1¼ teaspoons salt
¾   teaspoon caraway seeds, crushed
¼   teaspoon ground red pepper
1   can (15 ounces) no-salt-added diced tomatoes
2   teaspoons whole wheat flour
¾   cup reduced-fat sour cream, divided
1   tablespoon chopped fresh dill (optional)

1. Warm the oil in a large skillet over medium-high heat. Cook the chicken for 3 minutes, stirring occasionally, or until no longer pink. With a slotted spoon, transfer the chicken to a plate.

2. Add the onion, bell peppers, and wine to the skillet. Reduce the heat to medium-low, cover, and simmer for 10 minutes, stirring occasionally, or until the vegetables are very tender. Stir in the paprika, salt, caraway seeds, and ground red pepper. Cook, stirring, for 1 minute, or until fragrant. Add the tomatoes and bring to a boil. Reduce the heat to medium-low, cover, and simmer for 10 minutes, or until the flavors are blended.

3. In a small bowl, whisk together the flour and ½ cup of the sour cream. Return the chicken and any accumulated juices to the skillet. Add the sour cream mixture and cook for 3 minutes, stirring occasionally, or until the chicken is heated through and the sauce begins to thicken. Stir in the dill, if desired, and serve with the remaining sour cream.

Per serving: 317 calories ► 28 g protein ► 18 g carbohydrates ► 12 g fat ► 4 g saturated fat ► 5 g fiber ► 780 mg sodium

FRENCH CHICKEN AND LEEKS

Leeks often contain sand in between their layers. To clean them, trim away most of the dark green tops and roots, leaving the root end intact to hold the layers together. Slice the leek lengthwise to within 1" of the root end. Hold the leek by the root end, fan open the layers, and rinse thoroughly under cold running water.

Prep time: 15 minutes
Total time: 35 minutes
Makes 4 servings

- 1 tablespoon olive oil
- 1¼ pounds chicken cutlets
- 2 large leeks (white and light green parts only), sliced
- 2 yellow squash, sliced
- 1 Granny Smith apple, thinly sliced
- ½ cup white wine
- 1 tablespoon chopped fresh tarragon
- 1 teaspoon salt
- ½ cup reduced-fat sour cream
- 1 tablespoon Dijon mustard

1. Warm the oil in a large nonstick skillet over medium-high heat. Cook the chicken for 6 minutes, turning once, or until cooked through. Transfer the chicken to a plate.

2. Reduce the heat to medium. Add the leeks to the skillet and cook for 3 minutes, stirring occasionally, or until softened. Add the squash and apple. Cook for 5 minutes, stirring occasionally, or until softened. Add the wine, tarragon, and salt. Cover and cook for 5 minutes, or until the squash and apple are tender.

3. Return the chicken and any accumulated juices to the skillet. Stir in the sour cream and mustard and cook for 2 minutes, or until heated through.

Per serving: 325 calories ▸ 33 g protein ▸ 19 g carbohydrates ▸ 11 g fat ▸ 3.5 g saturated fat ▸ 2 g fiber ▸ 860 mg sodium

BALSAMIC CHICKEN WITH PEARS

Pears are best purchased while still firm. They will ripen in a day or two on a counter at room temperature. To avoid ending up with overripe pears, buy just what you need and use within a day or two.

Prep time: 15 minutes
Total time: 30 minutes
Makes 4 servings

- 4 boneless, skinless chicken breast halves
- ½ teaspoon dried thyme
- ½ teaspoon salt
- ¼ teaspoon ground black pepper
- 2 tablespoons olive oil
- ½ red onion, chopped
- 2 firm-ripe pears, cored and cut into thick slices
- ¾ cup low-sodium chicken broth
- 2 tablespoons balsamic vinegar
- 1 teaspoon arrowroot

1. Sprinkle the chicken with the thyme, salt, and pepper. Warm the oil in a large skillet over medium-high heat. Cook the chicken for 6 minutes, turning once, or until browned. Transfer the chicken to a plate.

2. Add the onion to the skillet and cook for 2 minutes, stirring frequently, or until softened. Add the pears and cook for 3 minutes, stirring occasionally, or until browned. In a small bowl, whisk together the broth, vinegar, and arrowroot. Stir into the skillet and cook for 1 minute, stirring, or until the sauce bubbles and thickens. Return the chicken and any accumulated juices to the skillet and cook for 2 minutes, or until a thermometer inserted in the thickest portion of the chicken registers 165°F and the juices run clear.

Per serving: 296 calories ▶ 32 g protein ▶ 18 g carbohydrates ▶ 11 g fat ▶ 2 g saturated fat ▶ 3 g fiber ▶ 472 mg sodium

JERK CHICKEN KEBABS

Many bottled jerk seasonings are loaded with sugar. Making your own not only tastes fresher, but you can control the amount of salt and sugar.

Prep time: 25 minutes
Total time: 35 minutes
Makes 4 servings

3   tablespoons red wine vinegar, divided
2   tablespoons canola oil
1   tablespoon Worcestershire sauce
1   tablespoon grated fresh ginger
2   scallions, finely chopped
1   teaspoon dried thyme
¾   teaspoon ground allspice
¾   teaspoon salt
¼   teaspoon ground red pepper
1   pound boneless, skinless chicken breasts, cut into 1" pieces
2   bell peppers, cut into 1" pieces
½   fresh pineapple, chopped (about 2 cups)
1   small red onion, finely chopped

1. In a large bowl, stir together 1 tablespoon of the vinegar, the oil, Worcestershire, ginger, scallions, thyme, allspice, salt, and ground red pepper. Add the chicken, tossing to coat. Thread the chicken and bell peppers on four 10" skewers.

2. Coat a grill rack or grill pan with cooking spray and preheat to medium. Grill the skewers for 8 minutes, turning once, or until the chicken is no longer pink and the juices run clear.

3. Meanwhile, in a medium bowl, toss together the pineapple, onion, and the remaining 2 tablespoons vinegar. Serve the salad with the skewers.

Per serving: 260 calories ▶ 25 g protein ▶ 17 g carbohydrates ▶ 10 g fat ▶ 1 g saturated fat ▶ 3 g fiber ▶ 615 mg sodium

LIME CHICKEN WITH CUCUMBER RELISH

This chicken pairs beautifully with the Quinoa with Green Chiles (page 205).

Prep time: 20 minutes
Total time: 30 minutes
Makes 4 servings

1   cucumber, peeled, seeded, and diced
¼   red onion, finely chopped
2   tablespoons rice wine vinegar
1   tablespoon canola oil
¼   teaspoon salt
⅛   teaspoon red-pepper flakes
2   tablespoons creamy natural peanut butter
2   tablespoons reduced-sodium soy sauce, divided
1   tablespoon fresh lime juice
2   teaspoons grated fresh ginger, divided
1   teaspoon Sucanat
2   teaspoons grated lime peel
1   clove garlic, minced
4   boneless, skinless chicken breast halves

1. In a large bowl, toss together the cucumber, onion, vinegar, oil, salt, and red-pepper flakes until well combined. Set the relish aside.

2. In a small bowl, stir together the peanut butter, 1 tablespoon of the soy sauce, the lime juice, 1 teaspoon of the ginger, the Sucanat, and 1 teaspoon hot water until blended and smooth. Set the peanut sauce aside.

3. In a pie plate, stir together the lime peel, garlic, the remaining 1 tablespoon soy sauce, and the remaining 1 teaspoon ginger. Add the chicken, turning to coat both sides.

4. Coat a nonstick grill pan with cooking spray and heat over medium-high heat. Grill the chicken for 6 minutes, turning once, or until a thermometer inserted in the thickest portion registers 165°F and the juices run clear. Serve with the cucumber relish and peanut sauce.

Per serving: 262 calories ▶ 33 g protein ▶ 6 g carbohydrates ▶ 11 g fat ▶ 1.5 g saturated fat ▶ 1 g fiber ▶ 579 mg sodium

TOMATO-BASIL CHICKEN

Tucking fresh herbs under the skin of chicken breasts adds an amazing amount of flavor. Use this low-carb dish as a sugar blocker for the Pasta with Gorgonzola Sauce and Pine Nuts (page 199), Spaghetti Duo with Asiago and Scallions (page 202), or the Farfalle with Asparagus, Goat Cheese, and Walnuts (page 198).

Prep time: 15 minutes
Total time: 50 minutes
Makes 4 servings

- 1 lemon
- 4 bone-in, skin-on chicken breast halves
- 8 fresh basil leaves + 1/4 cup chopped fresh basil
- 2 tablespoons olive oil, divided
- 1/2 teaspoon salt, divided
- 1/4 teaspoon ground black pepper
- 2 large tomatoes, chopped
- 1 tablespoon red wine vinegar
- 1 1/2 teaspoons Dijon mustard

1. Preheat the oven to 400°F. Coat a 13" × 9" baking pan with cooking spray.

2. Grate 1 teaspoon of the peel from the lemon; juice one half and cut the remaining half into 4 slices. With your fingers, carefully loosen the skin from the breast of the chicken. Tuck 2 basil leaves under the skin of each breast. Place the chicken in the baking dish. Drizzle with 1 tablespoon of the oil and sprinkle with 1/4 teaspoon of the salt and the pepper. Place the lemon slices over the chicken. Bake for 35 minutes, basting occasionally with the pan juices, or until a thermometer inserted in the thickest portion (not touching the bone) registers 170°F.

3. Meanwhile, in a large bowl, combine the tomatoes, vinegar, mustard, lemon juice, lemon peel, the remaining 1 tablespoon oil, and remaining 1/4 teaspoon salt. Stir in the chopped basil and toss to coat well.

4. Divide the chicken among 4 plates and top with the tomato mixture.

Per serving: 450 calories ▸ 45 g protein ▸ 6 g carbohydrates ▸ 27 g fat ▸ 6.5 g saturated fat ▸ 2 g fiber ▸ 480 mg sodium

CHICKEN WITH GREEN OLIVE SAUCE

The delicious combination of sweet, tart, and savory flavors makes this dish perfect for a quick weeknight meal. Serve with quinoa to round out the meal.

Prep time: 15 minutes
Total time: 1 hour
Makes 4 servings

---

1 teaspoon ground cumin
1 teaspoon smoked paprika
½ teaspoon salt
¼ teaspoon ground black pepper
4 large bone-in, skinless chicken thighs
2 tablespoons olive oil
1 onion, sliced
¾ cup low-sodium chicken broth
2 cloves garlic, minced
½ cup small pimiento-stuffed green olives
2 tablespoons sherry vinegar
2 navel oranges, peeled and cut crosswise into ½"-thick slices

1. In a cup, mix together the cumin, paprika, salt, and pepper. Sprinkle all over the chicken.

2. Warm the oil in a large nonstick skillet over medium heat. Cook the chicken for 4 minutes, turning, or until browned. Add the onion and cook for 4 minutes, or until softened. Add the broth and garlic. Bring to a boil. Reduce the heat to medium-low, cover, and simmer for 25 minutes, or until a thermometer inserted in a thigh registers 165°F and the juices run clear.

3. Stir in the olives and vinegar. Increase the heat to medium-high and cook for 3 minutes, stirring, or until the pan juices begin to thicken. Stir in the oranges and cook for 1 minute to heat through.

....

Per serving: 366 calories ▶ 36 g protein ▶ 16 g carbohydrates ▶ 17 g fat
▶ 3 g saturated fat ▶ 2 g fiber ▶ 861 mg sodium

TEX-MEX TURKEY BURGERS

Before grilling, and for best flavor, cover and refrigerate the burgers for at least 1 hour or up to overnight to
allow the flavors to blend.

Prep time: 15 minutes
Total time: 30 minutes
Makes 4 servings

1¼ pounds lean ground turkey
3   tablespoons chopped fresh cilantro
1   tablespoon salsa
½   fresh jalapeño chile pepper, finely chopped (wear plastic gloves when handling)
1   teaspoon chili powder
½   teaspoon ground cumin
½   teaspoon salt
1¼ cups shredded part-skim Colby-Jack cheese, divided
2   low-carb whole wheat hamburger buns, split
4   leaves lettuce
4   slices tomato

1. In a large bowl, mix together the turkey, cilantro, salsa, jalapeño, chili powder, cumin, salt, and ½ cup of the cheese. Form the mixture into 4 patties.

2. Coat a nonstick grill pan with cooking spray and heat over medium-high heat. Grill the burgers for 12 minutes, turning once, or until a thermometer inserted in the center registers 165°F and the meat is no longer pink. During the last minute of cooking, top each burger with the remaining cheese.

3. Divide the buns among 4 plates. Top each with a burger, lettuce, and tomato.

Per serving: 319 calories ▶ 46 g protein ▶ 14 g carbohydrates ▶ 9 g fat
▶ 4.5 g saturated fat ▶ 3 g fiber ▶ 796 mg sodium

TURKEY PICADILLO MEATBALLS

The bread crumbs typically added to meatballs and meat loaf (to keep them from becoming too dry and dense) are laden with carbs and unnecessary sodium, so to reduce both, flaxseed meal is substituted.

Prep time: 25 minutes
Total time: 55 minutes
Makes 4 servings

- 1 pound lean ground turkey
- ½ cup ground flaxseeds
- ⅓ cup chopped fresh cilantro
- 1 large egg
- 1 teaspoon ground cumin, divided
- ½ teaspoon salt, divided
- ¼ teaspoon ground black pepper
- 2 tablespoons olive oil
- 1 onion, chopped
- 1 green bell pepper, chopped
- 2 cloves garlic, minced
- 1 can (14.5 ounces) no-salt-added diced tomatoes
- ¼ cup sliced pimiento-stuffed green olives
- 2 tablespoons raisins
- 2 tablespoons red wine vinegar

1. In a large bowl, stir together the turkey, ground flaxseeds, cilantro, egg, ½ teaspoon of the cumin, ¼ teaspoon of the salt, and the black pepper until well blended. Form the mixture into 12 meatballs.

2. Warm the oil in a large, deep nonstick skillet over medium-high heat. Cook the meatballs for 8 minutes, turning occasionally, or until browned. Transfer to a plate.

3. Add the onion, bell pepper, and garlic to the skillet and cook for 5 minutes, stirring occasionally, or until tender. Add the tomatoes, olives, raisins, vinegar, the remaining ½ teaspoon cumin, and remaining ¼ teaspoon salt. Bring to a boil. Return the meatballs to the skillet. Reduce the heat to medium-low, cover, and simmer for 15 minutes, stirring occasionally, or until the meatballs are no longer pink.

....

Per serving: 374 calories ▸ 25 g protein ▸ 18 g carbohydrates ▸ 23 g fat ▸ 3.5 g saturated fat ▸ 6 g fiber ▸ 584 mg sodium

SPICY TURKEY WITH PEANUTS

The ribs and seeds of the jalapeño chiles are where the heat is. If you like it spicy, leave them in. Serve with cooked brown rice.

Prep time: 20 minutes
Total time: 30 minutes
Makes 4 servings

4 tablespoons canola oil, divided
1½ pounds turkey cutlets, cut into ½" strips
2 tablespoons reduced-sodium soy sauce
2 tablespoons fresh lime juice
2 teaspoons fish sauce
2 teaspoons Sucanat
2 shallots, finely chopped
⅓ cup salted dry-roasted peanuts, finely chopped
1 jalapeño chile pepper, seeded and finely chopped (wear plastic gloves when handling)
¼ cup chopped fresh basil
¼ cup chopped fresh cilantro

1. Heat 2 tablespoons of the oil in a large nonstick skillet over medium-high heat. Cook the turkey for 5 minutes, stirring frequently, or until browned and no longer pink. Transfer the turkey to a plate.

2. Meanwhile, in a small bowl, whisk together the soy sauce, lime juice, fish sauce, and Sucanat.

3. Add the remaining 2 tablespoons oil to the skillet and heat over medium heat. Cook the shallots, peanuts, and jalapeño for 1 minute, stirring, or until fragrant. Add the soy sauce mixture and bring to a simmer. Return the turkey and any accumulated juices to the skillet and cook for 1 minute, stirring frequently, or until heated through. Remove from the heat. Stir in the basil and cilantro.

Per serving: 385 calories ▸ 40 g protein ▸ 13 g carbohydrates ▸ 21 g fat ▸ 2 g saturated fat ▸ 1 g fiber ▸ 701 mg sodium

ZUCCHINI LASAGNA

Here's a perfect starch blocker—zucchini substitutes for high-GL pasta in this classic dish. So delicious you'll never miss the pasta.

Prep time: 15 minutes
Total time: 1 hour
Makes 6 servings

1¼ pounds ground turkey
2 cups no-sugar-added marinara sauce, divided
4 medium zucchini (1½ pounds total)
1 cup part-skim ricotta cheese
1 cup shredded part-skim mozzarella cheese
¼ cup grated Parmesan cheese

1. Preheat the oven to 375°F. Coat a 9" × 9" baking pan with cooking spray.

2. Coat a large nonstick skillet with cooking spray and heat over medium-high heat. Cook the turkey for 5 minutes, breaking up the meat with a wooden spoon, or until no longer pink. Add 1½ cups of the marinara. Cook for 1 minute and remove from the heat.

3. Cut the zucchini lengthwise into ¼"-thick slices. Place one-third of the zucchini in the bottom of the baking pan. Spread with half of the turkey mixture. Spoon ½ cup of the ricotta over the turkey and sprinkle with ½ cup of the mozzarella. Repeat the layering with another one-third of the zucchini and the remaining turkey mixture, ricotta, and mozzarella. Top with the remaining zucchini and spread with the remaining ½ cup marinara. Sprinkle with the Parmesan cheese.

4. Bake, uncovered, for 45 minutes, or until hot and bubbling. Let stand for 10 minutes before cutting.

Per serving: 278 calories ▶ 36 g protein ▶ 13 g carbohydrates ▶ 10 g fat ▶ 5 g saturated fat ▶ 3 g fiber ▶ 689 mg sodium

SHRIMP SCAMPI PASTA

Be sure to serve this meal after a carb-blocking first course such as nuts and wine.

Prep time: 20 minutes
Total time: 35 minutes
Makes 4 servings

4   ounces whole grain rotini pasta
3   cups broccoli florets
2   cups cauliflower florets
2   tablespoons extra-virgin olive oil, divided
1   pound peeled and deveined large shrimp
2   cups grape tomatoes
4   cloves garlic, thinly sliced
1   tablespoon capers, rinsed
2   tablespoons butter, at room temperature
1   teaspoon grated lemon peel
1   tablespoon fresh lemon juice
½   teaspoon salt
¼   cup chopped fresh flat-leaf parsley

1. Prepare the pasta according to package directions, adding the broccoli and cauliflower during the last 3 minutes of cooking time. Drain, reserving ¼ cup of the cooking water.

2. Meanwhile, heat 1 tablespoon of the oil in a large, deep nonstick skillet over medium-high heat. Cook the shrimp for 3 minutes, turning once, or until just opaque. Transfer to a plate.

3. Add the remaining 1 tablespoon oil to the skillet and heat over medium-high heat. Cook the tomatoes, garlic, and capers for 3 minutes, or until the tomatoes just begin to burst. Swirl in the butter until blended.

4. Add the drained pasta mixture, the shrimp, lemon peel, lemon juice, and salt, and cook for 1 minute, or until hot. Stir in the parsley.

Per serving: 394 calories ▸ 31 g protein ▸ 32 g carbohydrates ▸ 16 g fat ▸ 5 g saturated fat ▸ 5 g fiber ▸ 505 mg sodium

SCALLOPS WITH BACON AND APPLE

To make sure the scallops brown properly, pat them dry with paper towels before you cook them.

Prep time: 15 minutes
Total time: 40 minutes
Makes 4 servings

- 3 slices bacon
- 1 pound sea scallops
- 2 Golden Delicious apples, peeled and thickly sliced
- ½ cup heavy cream
- 1 tablespoon apple cider vinegar
- ¼ teaspoon salt
- ¼ teaspoon ground black pepper
- 2 tablespoons snipped fresh chives

1. Heat a large nonstick skillet over medium-high heat. Cook the bacon for 4 to 5 minutes, or until crisp. Transfer to a paper towel–lined plate. Pour off the drippings and reserve. Crumble the bacon.

2. Return 1 tablespoon of the drippings to the skillet and heat over medium-high heat. Cook the scallops for 3 minutes, turning once, or until browned. Transfer to a plate.

3. Add the remaining drippings to the skillet over medium heat. Cook the apples for 5 minutes, stirring occasionally, or until lightly browned. Stir in the cream and any accumulated liquid from the scallops. Simmer for 3 minutes, stirring occasionally, or until the cream reduces and begins to thicken slightly.

4. Add the scallops, vinegar, salt, and pepper to the skillet and cook for 1 minute, or until hot. Stir in the bacon and the chives.

Per serving: 321 calories ▶ 22 g protein ▶ 14 g carbohydrates ▶ 20 g fat ▶ 9.5 g saturated fat ▶ 1 g fiber ▶ 481 mg sodium

ROASTED SPICED SALMON

You can use salmon steaks instead of fillets: They will take longer to roast, so test them after 20 minutes.

Prep time: 10 minutes
Total time: 25 minutes
Makes 4 servings

- 1 tablespoon chili powder
- 1 tablespoon olive oil
- 1 teaspoon Sucanat
- ½ teaspoon ground cumin
- ½ teaspoon dried thyme
- ¼ teaspoon salt
- ¼ teaspoon ground black pepper
- 4 salmon fillets (6 ounces each)
  Lemon wedges, for serving (optional)

1. Preheat the oven to 400°F. Coat a 13" × 9" baking dish with cooking spray.

2. In a cup, mix the chili powder, oil, Sucanat, cumin, thyme, salt, and pepper. Rub all over the fillets. Place the fillets in the baking dish and roast for 15 minutes, or until the fish is opaque. Serve with lemon wedges, if desired.

Per serving: 283 calories ▶ 34 g protein ▶ 2 g carbohydrates ▶ 15 g fat ▶ 2 g saturated fat ▶ 1 g fiber ▶ 241 mg sodium

SICILIAN TILAPIA

If you aren't a fennel fan, you may use 2 ribs of chopped celery instead.

Prep time: 15 minutes
Total time: 35 minutes
Makes 4 servings

- 2 tablespoons olive oil
- 1 bulb fennel, coarsely chopped
- 3 cloves garlic, minced
- 1 can (14.5 ounces) no-salt-added diced tomatoes
- 1 tablespoon red wine vinegar
- 1 tablespoon capers, rinsed
- 1 tablespoon golden raisins, chopped
- 8 kalamata olives, pitted and chopped
- ¼ teaspoon salt
- 1 pound tilapia fillets
- ¼ cup thinly sliced fresh basil

1. Warm the oil in a large nonstick skillet over medium-high heat. Cook the fennel for 3 minutes, stirring frequently, or until softened. Stir in the garlic and cook for 1 minute. Add the tomatoes, vinegar, capers, raisins, olives, and salt. Reduce the heat to medium-low, cover, and simmer for 5 minutes, stirring occasionally, or until the mixture thickens slightly.

2. Add the fillets to the skillet, pushing them down into the sauce and spooning some sauce on top. Reduce the heat to low, cover, and simmer for 8 minutes, or until the fish flakes easily. Sprinkle with the basil.

Per serving: 239 calories ► 25 g protein ► 12 g carbohydrates ► 11 g fat ► 2 g saturated fat ► 3 g fiber ► 432 mg sodium

ROASTED HADDOCK
WITH ORANGE-OLIVE SALSA

Try this salsa with fresh fennel instead of the celery. If you have grapefruit on hand, substitute half a large grapefruit for one of the oranges.

Prep time: 20 minutes
Total time: 35 minutes
Makes 4 servings

4   haddock or cod fillets (6 ounces each)
½   teaspoon salt, divided
3   navel oranges
½   cup pitted green olives, slivered
¼   cup chopped fresh mint
1   rib celery, chopped
1   tablespoon extra-virgin olive oil
2   teaspoons red wine vinegar

1. Preheat the oven to 400°F. Coat a small shallow roasting pan with cooking spray. Sprinkle the fillets with ¼ teaspoon of the salt and place in the pan. Roast for 15 minutes, or until the fish flakes easily.

2. Meanwhile, grate the peel from 1 orange into a large bowl. With a small knife, cut away the peel and white pith from all of the oranges. Coarsely chop the flesh and add to the bowl. Add the olives, mint, celery, oil, vinegar, and remaining ¼ teaspoon salt. Toss well to combine. Serve with the fillets.

Per serving: 260 calories ▶ 34 g protein ▶ 15 g carbohydrates ▶ 7 g fat ▶ 1 g saturated fat ▶ 3 g fiber ▶ 623 mg sodium

CORNMEAL-CRUSTED CATFISH

Use this tasty coating on any firm-fleshed fish, such as cod or red snapper fillets. If you don't have buttermilk on hand, stir together ¾ cup 2% milk and 1 tablespoon distilled white vinegar. Serve the fish with lemon wedges and tartar sauce.

Prep time: 10 minutes
Total time: 50 minutes + marinating time
Makes 4 servings

¾ cup buttermilk
4 catfish fillets (6 ounces each)
1 large egg
⅔ cup yellow cornmeal
1 teaspoon crab-boil seasoning
½ teaspoon smoked paprika
¼ teaspoon salt
2 tablespoons canola oil

1. Pour the buttermilk into a large resealable plastic food storage bag. Add the fillets, squeeze out the air, and seal the bag; turn to coat the fillets. Refrigerate, turning the bag occasionally, for at least 30 minutes or up to 2 hours.

2. In a shallow bowl or pie plate, whisk the egg. In another shallow bowl or plate, combine the cornmeal, seasoning, paprika, and salt. Lift the fillets out of the marinade (discard the marinade). Working with 1 fillet at a time, dip into the egg, shaking off the excess, then dredge in the cornmeal mixture to coat.

3. Warm the oil in a large nonstick skillet over medium heat. Cook the fillets for 10 minutes, turning once, or until the coating is golden brown and the fish flakes easily.

Per serving: 343 calories ▶ 39 g protein ▶ 18 g carbohydrates ▶ 13 g fat ▶ 2.5 g saturated fat ▶ 1 g fiber ▶ 458 mg sodium

PAO-SPICED STIR-FRY WITH TOFU

Substitute celery for the bok choy to make this a speedy pantry meal. Serve with chopped cilantro and additional hot sauce for those who like it extra spicy.

Prep time: 15 minutes
Total time: 30 minutes
Makes 4 servings

- 1 tablespoon canola oil
- 1 package (16 ounces) frozen vegetables for stir-fry
- 4 cups sliced bok choy
- ¼ cup red wine vinegar
- 3 tablespoons hoisin sauce
- 1 tablespoon dry sherry or white wine
- 1 tablespoon grated fresh ginger
- 3-4 teaspoons Sriracha or hot-pepper sauce
- 2 teaspoons toasted sesame oil
- 1 package (7 ounces) baked tofu, cut into 1" pieces
- 1 can (8 ounces) sliced water chestnuts, drained
- ¼ cup unsalted dry-roasted peanuts, coarsely chopped

1. Warm the canola oil in a large nonstick skillet or wok over medium-high heat. Cook the frozen vegetables for 5 minutes, stirring occasionally, or until softened. Add the bok choy and cook for 6 minutes, stirring, or until tender-crisp.

2. Meanwhile, in a small bowl, whisk together the vinegar, hoisin sauce, sherry, ginger, Sriracha, and sesame oil.

3. Add the vinegar mixture, tofu, and water chestnuts to the skillet. Bring to a simmer and cook for 1 minute, or until heated through.

4. Serve sprinkled with the peanuts.

Per serving: 274 calories ▶ 12 g protein ▶ 25 g carbohydrates ▶ 14 g fat ▶ 1.5 g saturated fat ▶ 7 g fiber ▶ 405 mg sodium

EGGPLANT PARMESAN

Roasting eggplant takes much less time than breading and frying. It's lighter and tastes just as good.

Prep time: 20 minutes
Total time: 1 hour 15 minutes
Makes 6 servings

2   eggplants (1¼ pounds each), cut crosswise into ½"-thick slices
2   tablespoons olive oil, divided
2   cups reduced-sodium marinara sauce
8   tablespoons grated Parmesan cheese, divided
1½ cups shredded part-skim mozzarella cheese

1. Preheat the oven to 450°F. Brush 2 large baking sheets with 1 tablespoon of the oil. Arrange the eggplant slices in a single layer on the baking sheet and brush with the remaining 1 tablespoon oil. Roast for 15 minutes, or until tender. Reduce the oven temperature to 400°F.

2. Coat a shallow baking dish with cooking spray. Arrange half the eggplant in the dish, overlapping to fit if necessary. Spread with ³⁄₄ cup of the marinara. Sprinkle with 3 tablespoons of the Parmesan and ³⁄₄ cup of the mozzarella. Top with the remaining eggplant. Spread with the remaining marinara and sprinkle with the remaining mozzarella.

3. Cover the dish with foil and bake for 20 minutes, or until the filling is hot and the sauce is bubbling. Uncover and sprinkle with the remaining 5 tablespoons Parmesan. Bake for 15 minutes, or until the topping is browned. Let stand for 10 minutes before serving.

Per serving: 213 calories ▸ 12 g protein ▸ 16 g carbohydrates ▸ 12 g fat ▸ 4.5 g saturated fat ▸ 7 g fiber ▸ 347 mg sodium

CAULIFLOWER FRITTATA

Cauliflower acts as a starch mimic, replacing potatoes, which are commonly used in frittatas.

Prep time: 15 minutes
Total time: 45 minutes
Makes 4 servings

½ head cauliflower, broken into florets, cut into ½" slices
8 large eggs
⅓ cup grated Romano or Parmesan cheese, divided
¼ cup half-and-half
3 tablespoons chopped fresh parsley
¼ teaspoon salt
1 tablespoon olive oil
1 red onion, chopped

1. Preheat the oven to 375°F.

2. In a large ovenproof nonstick skillet, bring 2 cups of water to a boil. Cook the cauliflower for 2 minutes, or until tender-crisp. Drain well. Wipe the skillet clean.

3. Meanwhile, in a large bowl, whisk together the eggs, ¼ cup of the cheese, the half-and-half, parsley, and salt.

4. Warm the oil in the same skillet over medium-high heat. Cook the onion for 5 minutes, stirring occasionally, or until softened. Stir in the cauliflower. Pour the egg mixture over the vegetables, stirring to combine. Cook over medium heat for 3 minutes, or until the mixture just begins to set.

5. Sprinkle with the remaining cheese and bake for 15 minutes, or until set.

Per serving: 257 calories ▸ 17 g protein ▸ 8 g carbohydrates ▸ 18 g fat ▸ 6 g saturated fat ▸ 2 g fiber ▸ 458 mg sodium

SIDE DISHES

FARFALLE WITH ASPARAGUS, GOAT CHEESE, AND WALNUTS

Olive oil, goat cheese, and walnuts all combine to block the starch in the pasta in this recipe.

Prep time: 10 minutes
Total time: 25 minutes
Makes 4 servings

4 ounces whole grain farfalle (bow-tie) pasta
¾ pound asparagus, cut into 1" pieces
2 tablespoons olive oil
½ red onion, thinly sliced
¼ teaspoon salt
⅛ teaspoon ground black pepper
1½ ounces goat cheese
⅓ cup walnuts, toasted and coarsely chopped

1. Prepare the pasta according to package directions, adding the asparagus during the last 2 minutes of cooking time. Drain, reserving ¼ cup of the cooking water.

2. In the pasta cooking pot, warm the oil over medium heat. Cook the onion for 5 minutes, stirring occasionally, or until softened.

3. Stir in the drained pasta, reserved pasta cooking water, the asparagus, salt, and pepper. Cook for 1 minute, stirring, or until heated through. Remove from the heat and stir in the goat cheese.

4. Serve sprinkled with the walnuts.

Per serving: 272 calories ▸ 10 g protein ▸ 25 g carbohydrates ▸ 16 g fat ▸ 3 g saturated fat ▸ 5 g fiber ▸ 200 mg sodium

PASTA WITH GORGONZOLA SAUCE AND PINE NUTS

If you like, sprinkle the pasta with 3 tablespoons of crisp-cooked crumbled prosciutto.

Prep time: 10 minutes
Total time: 20 minutes
Makes 4 servings

- 4 ounces whole wheat rotini pasta
- 2 cups broccoli florets, coarsely chopped
- ¾ cup half-and-half
- 1 clove garlic, minced
- ⅓ cup crumbled Gorgonzola cheese
- ¼ cup pine nuts, toasted
- ¼ teaspoon salt
- ⅛ teaspoon ground black pepper

1. Prepare the pasta according to package directions, adding the broccoli during the last 2 minutes of cooking time. Drain.

2. In the pasta cooking pot, combine the half-and-half and garlic and bring to a boil over medium-high heat. Reduce the heat to medium. Add the cheese and cook for 1 minute, stirring, or until the sauce begins to thicken. Stir in the pasta, broccoli, pine nuts, salt, and pepper. Cook for 1 minute, tossing to coat well, or until heated through.

Per serving: 264 calories ▶ 10 g protein ▶ 24 g carbohydrates ▶ 15 g fat ▶ 6 g saturated fat ▶ 6 g fiber ▶ 308 mg sodium

MEXICAN PASTA AND BEANS

Small pastas (called mini or piccolini) are now available in a wide variety of shapes, including penne, fusilli, farfalle, wheels, or ziti. Any of them will work nicely here in place of the small shells.

Prep time: 10 minutes
Total time: 25 minutes
Makes 4 servings

- 1 cup whole wheat small shell pasta
- 1 tablespoon olive oil
- 1 green bell pepper, chopped
- 3 scallions, sliced
- 2 teaspoons chili powder
- 1 cup canned no-salt-added black soybeans, rinsed and drained
- ¾ cup mild salsa
- 2 tablespoons chopped fresh cilantro

1. Prepare the pasta according to package directions. Drain.

2. Meanwhile, warm the oil in a large nonstick skillet over medium-high heat. Cook the bell pepper for 5 minutes, stirring occasionally, or until softened. Add the scallions and chili powder and cook for 1 minute, stirring, or until fragrant.

3. Stir in the pasta, beans, salsa, and cilantro. Cook for 1 minute, or until hot.

Per serving: 217 calories ► 10 g protein ► 31 g carbohydrates ► 7 g fat ► 1 g saturated fat ► 9 g fiber ► 226 mg sodium

DITALINI WITH SPINACH AND RICOTTA

If you prefer more of a peppery bite, use baby arugula instead of the spinach.

Prep time: 15 minutes
Total time: 20 minutes
Makes 4 servings

1   cup ditalini or other small pasta
1   tablespoon olive oil
2   cloves garlic, minced
1   shallot, thinly sliced
¼   teaspoon red-pepper flakes
1   package (8 ounces) baby spinach
¼   teaspoon salt
½   cup part-skim ricotta cheese
6   soft sun-dried tomatoes, chopped
⅓   cup grated Parmesan cheese, divided

1. Prepare the pasta according to package directions. Drain, reserving ¼ cup of the cooking water.

2. In the pasta cooking pot, warm the oil over medium-high heat. Cook the garlic, shallot, and red-pepper flakes for 2 minutes, stirring, or until fragrant. Add the spinach and salt and cook for 3 minutes, stirring, or until the spinach just begins to wilt.

3. Stir in the pasta, reserved pasta cooking water, ricotta, sun-dried tomatoes, and 3 tablespoons of the Parmesan. Cook 1 minute, tossing to coat well, or until the pasta is hot.

4. Serve sprinkled with the remaining Parmesan.

Per serving: 251 calories ▶ 12 g protein ▶ 33 g carbohydrates ▶ 9 g fat ▶ 3.5 g saturated fat ▶ 4 g fiber ▶ 389 mg sodium

SPAGHETTI DUO WITH ASIAGO AND SCALLIONS

Spaghetti squash is a good alternative to pasta. The cooked flesh of this mild-flavored squash separates into long spaghetti-like strands. The larger the spaghetti squash, the thicker and more flavorful the strands.

Prep time: 10 minutes
Total time: 30 minutes
Makes 4 servings

1   medium spaghetti squash (about 2 pounds), halved lengthwise and seeded
4   ounces whole wheat thin spaghetti, broken
2   tablespoons unsalted butter
1   bunch scallions, thinly sliced
$\frac{1}{2}$ teaspoon red-pepper flakes
$\frac{1}{2}$ teaspoon salt
$\frac{1}{3}$ cup grated Asiago or Parmesan cheese, divided
$\frac{1}{4}$ cup chopped fresh parsley

1. Pierce the outside of the squash a few times with a fork. Place the squash cut side down in a large microwaveable baking dish. Pour $\frac{1}{4}$ cup water around the squash. Cover and microwave on high power for 10 to 15 minutes, or until very tender when pierced with a fork. Let cool for 10 minutes.

2. Meanwhile, prepare the pasta according to package directions. Drain.

3. In the pasta cooking pot, heat the butter over medium heat. Cook the scallions for 1 minute, stirring, or until softened. Add the red-pepper flakes and salt and cook for 1 minute, or until fragrant.

4. With a fork, scrape the spaghetti-like strands of squash into the pot. Stir in the pasta and half of the cheese. Cook for 1 to 2 minutes, stirring gently, or until hot.

5. Serve sprinkled with the parsley and the remaining cheese.

Per serving: 267 calories ▶ 8 g protein ▶ 40 g carbohydrates ▶ 11 g fat ▶ 5.5 g saturated fat ▶ 7 g fiber ▶ 429 mg sodium

SPAGHETTI SQUASH WITH CARAMELIZED ONIONS AND GOAT CHEESE

A pasta mimic, you can make spaghetti squash in a matter of minutes in a microwave. But if you prefer, you can roast the squash instead: Halve the squash lengthwise and scoop out the seeds. Coat a large roasting pan with cooking spray, place the squash cut side down, and roast in a 375°F oven for 35 to 40 minutes, or until fork-tender. This recipe is placed with the pasta dishes because this dish is similar to one made with pasta and will fit the bill when looking for a delicious pasta dish without any sugar spikes.

Prep time: 10 minutes
Total time: 25 minutes
Makes 4 servings

- 1 medium spaghetti squash (2 pounds), halved lengthwise and seeded
- 1½ tablespoons olive oil
- 1 large sweet onion, thinly sliced
- 1 large red bell pepper, cut into thin strips
- ⅓ cup pitted green olives, halved
- 1 teaspoon chopped fresh rosemary
- ¾ teaspoon salt
- 2 cups baby arugula
- ½ cup crumbled goat cheese

1. Pierce the outside of the squash a few times with a fork. Place the squash cut side down in a large microwaveable baking dish. Pour ¼ cup water around the squash. Cover and microwave on high power for 10 minutes, or until very tender when pierced with a fork. Let cool for 10 minutes.

2. Meanwhile, warm the oil in a large nonstick skillet over medium-high heat. Cook the onion and bell pepper for 8 minutes, stirring occasionally, or until tender. Add the olives, rosemary, and salt and cook for 1 minute, or until heated through.

3. With a fork, scrape the spaghetti-like strands of squash into the skillet. Cook for 2 minutes, stirring gently, or until heated through. Stir in the arugula just until wilted.

4. Serve sprinkled with the goat cheese.

Per serving: 254 calories ▶ 8 g protein ▶ 23 g carbohydrates ▶ 15 g fat ▶ 6 g saturated fat ▶ 2 g fiber ▶ 752 mg sodium

CREAMY BROWN RICE WITH MUSHROOMS

Here's a quick rice dish reminiscent of risotto but involving much less work. Serve with roast chicken or salmon after a first-course salad for the perfect sugar-blocker meal.

Prep time: 10 minutes
Total time: 25 minutes
Makes 4 servings

- 1 tablespoon olive oil
- 1 package (8 ounces) sliced cremini mushrooms
- 1 onion, finely chopped
- 1 cup low-sodium chicken broth
- ¾ cup quick-cooking brown rice
- ⅓ cup Italian cheese and herb cooking creme

1. Warm the oil in a large saucepan over medium-high heat. Cook the mushrooms and onion for 8 minutes, stirring occasionally, or until lightly browned.

2. Add the broth and rice and bring to a boil. Reduce the heat to medium-low, cover, and simmer for 10 minutes, stirring occasionally, or until the rice is tender.

3. Stir in the cooking creme and cook for 1 minute, or until heated through.

Per serving: 154 calories ▶ 4 g protein ▶ 17 g carbohydrates ▶ 9 g fat ▶ 3.5 g saturated fat ▶ 1 g fiber ▶ 113 mg sodium

QUINOA WITH GREEN CHILES

Quinoa comes in a variety of colors and is an excellent source of protein. Try a blend of red and black quinoa. It has a slightly nutty flavor and is a high-protein substitute for couscous or bulgur.

Prep time: 10 minutes
Total time: 35 minutes
Makes 4 servings

1   tablespoon canola oil
1   medium onion, chopped
1   clove garlic, minced
¾   teaspoon chili powder
¼   teaspoon salt
1   cup low-sodium chicken broth
½   cup quinoa, rinsed and drained
½   cup frozen corn kernels
1   can (4.5 ounces) chopped mild green chiles, drained

1. Warm the oil in a large nonstick skillet over medium-high heat. Cook the onion for 6 minutes, stirring occasionally, or until tender. Add the garlic, chili powder, and salt and cook for 1 minute, stirring, or until fragrant.

2. Add the broth and quinoa and bring to a boil. Reduce the heat, cover, and simmer for 15 minutes, or until the liquid is evaporated and the quinoa is tender.

3. Stir in the corn and chiles and cook for 2 minutes, stirring, or until heated through.

Per serving: 125 calories ▶ 4 g protein ▶ 18 g carbohydrates ▶ 5 g fat ▶ 0.5 g saturated fat ▶ 3 g fiber ▶ 299 mg sodium

CHEESY QUINOA AND KALE

Serve this nutrient-rich side dish with roast chicken or fish. If you prefer, you may use 2 cups chopped trimmed fresh kale instead of frozen.

Prep time: 10 minutes
Total time: 35 minutes
Makes 6 servings

1 tablespoon butter
1 cup quinoa, rinsed and drained
1 can (14.5 ounces) low-sodium chicken broth
½ package (10 ounces) frozen chopped kale
2 tablespoons apple cider vinegar
¾ teaspoon dried thyme
¼ teaspoon salt
¼ teaspoon ground black pepper
½ cup crumbled goat cheese
3 scallions, chopped
1 teaspoon grated lemon peel

1. Heat the butter in a medium saucepan over medium heat. Cook the quinoa for 5 minutes, stirring, or until lightly toasted. Stir in the broth, kale, vinegar, thyme, salt, and pepper. Bring to a boil. Reduce the heat to low, cover, and simmer for 15 minutes, or until the quinoa and kale are tender.

2. Stir in the goat cheese, scallions, and lemon peel and cook for 1 minute, or until heated through.

Per serving: 189 calories ▸ 9 g protein ▸ 21 g carbohydrates ▸ 8 g fat ▸ 4 g saturated fat ▸ 3 g fiber ▸ 189 mg sodium

FRUITY COUSCOUS

Turn this simple dish into a side for all seasons by changing a few ingredients. When the weather starts to cool, add a chopped pear, dried cranberries, and crunchy walnuts for a toasty autumn side. For lighter summer fare, add chopped nectarines or peaches, toasted pine nuts, and chopped fresh mint. Be sure to eat with meat, poultry, or fish after a salad tossed with vinaigrette.

Prep time: 10 minutes
Total time: 20 minutes
Makes 6 servings

- 1 tablespoon canola oil
- 1 apple, peeled and coarsely chopped
- 1 small onion, finely chopped
- 1¼ cups low-sodium chicken broth
- ¼ cup dried apricots, chopped
- ¼ teaspoon salt
- ¾ cup whole wheat couscous
- 3 tablespoons slivered almonds, toasted

1. Warm the oil in a medium saucepan over medium-high heat. Cook the apple and onion for 4 minutes, stirring occasionally, or until lightly browned.

2. Add the broth, apricots, and salt and bring to a boil. Remove from the heat and stir in the couscous. Cover and let stand for 5 minutes, or until the liquid is absorbed. Fluff the couscous with a fork and stir in the almonds.

Per serving: 142 calories ▸ 4 g protein ▸ 22 g carbohydrates ▸ 5 g fat ▸ 0.5 g saturated fat ▸ 4 g fiber ▸ 112 mg sodium

BULGUR PILAF WITH WILD RICE

This dish pairs well with Lime Chicken with Cucumber Relish (page 180) or Roasted Spiced Salmon (page 189). Cooking the wild rice and bulgur in a plentiful amount of boiling water, just like pasta, removes some of the starch and is a sugar-blocking technique.

Prep time: 10 minutes
Total time: 1 hour
Makes 6 servings

½ cup wild rice
½ cup bulgur
2 tablespoons butter
1 scallion, chopped
1 tomato, chopped
2 tablespoons chopped fresh basil
¼ teaspoon salt

1. Bring a large pot of water to a boil. Add the wild rice. Reduce the heat to medium, cover, and simmer for 30 minutes, or until almost tender. Add the bulgur and simmer for 15 minutes, or until both of the grains are tender. Drain.

2. In the same pot, heat the butter over medium heat. Cook the scallion for 1 minute, stirring, or until soft. Return the rice mixture to the pan. Stir in the tomato, basil, and salt and cook for 1 minute, or until heated through.

....

Per serving: 126 calories ▸ 4 g protein ▸ 20 g carbohydrates ▸ 6 g fat ▸ 3.5 g saturated fat ▸ 3 g fiber ▸ 102 mg sodium

BULGUR WITH PISTACHIOS

Adding nuts to grain dishes helps block the starch in the dish. Always serve alongside protein such as grilled steak, chicken, or pork—or even with a burger.

Prep time: 15 minutes
Total time: 45 minutes
Makes 8 servings

- 1 tablespoon olive oil
- 1 onion, finely chopped
- 2 carrots, shredded
- ¼ teaspoon ground cinnamon
- ¼ teaspoon ground allspice
- ⅛ teaspoon ground red pepper
- 1 can (15 ounces) low-sodium chicken broth
- 1 cup bulgur
- ¼ teaspoon salt
- 1 tablespoon sherry vinegar
- 3 tablespoons chopped pistachios

1. Warm the oil in a large saucepan over medium-high heat. Cook the onion and carrots for 5 minutes, or until softened. Add the cinnamon, allspice, and ground red pepper and cook for 1 minute, stirring, or until fragrant. Add the broth, bulgur, and salt. Reduce the heat to low, cover, and simmer for 15 minutes, or until the liquid is absorbed. Remove from the heat and let stand, covered, for 5 minutes.

2. Stir in the vinegar and serve sprinkled with the pistachios.

Per serving: 114 calories ▶ 4 g protein ▶ 17 g carbohydrates ▶ 4 g fat ▶ 0.5 g saturated fat ▶ 4 g fiber ▶ 250 mg sodium

CHUNKY GARLIC MASHED POTATOES

Replacing half of the potatoes with cauliflower is a starch-mimicking technique that reduces the glycemic load.

Prep time: 15 minutes
Total time: 30 minutes
Makes 4 servings

- ½ head cauliflower, cut into florets
- 2 medium baking potatoes, peeled and cut into 1" pieces
- 4 cloves garlic, sliced
- ¼ cup whole milk
- 3 tablespoons butter, softened
- ½ teaspoon salt
- ⅛ teaspoon ground black pepper

In a large saucepan, combine the cauliflower, potatoes, garlic, and enough water to cover by 2". Bring to a boil over high heat. Reduce the heat to medium-low, cover, and simmer for 15 minutes, or until tender. Drain and return to the pot. Add the milk, butter, salt, and pepper and mash with a potato masher until smooth.

Per serving: 185 calories ▸ 3 g protein ▸ 23 g carbohydrates ▸ 9 g fat ▸ 6 g saturated fat ▸ 3 g fiber ▸ 311 mg sodium

RED POTATOES WITH DILL AND SCALLIONS

If you can't find baby red potatoes, use smaller red potatoes and cut them into quarters.

Prep time: 10 minutes
Total time: 25 minutes
Makes 4 servings

1¼ pounds baby red potatoes, halved
2 tablespoons white wine vinegar
2 tablespoons chopped fresh dill
2 scallions, thinly sliced
1 tablespoon olive oil
½ teaspoon salt
¼ teaspoon ground black pepper
¼ cup sour cream

In a large saucepan, combine the potatoes with enough cold water to cover by 2". Bring to a boil over high heat. Reduce the heat to medium, cover, and simmer for 15 minutes, or until tender. Drain and return to the pot. Place over low heat and add the vinegar, dill, scallions, oil, salt, and pepper. Toss to coat well. Remove from the heat. Serve with the sour cream.

Per serving: 155 calories ▸ 3 g protein ▸ 24 g carbohydrates ▸ 6 g fat ▸ 2 g saturated fat ▸ 3 g fiber ▸ 310 mg sodium

BUTTER-ROASTED SWEET POTATOES

Roasting sweet potatoes caramelizes them, making them naturally sweet, and cooking them in butter blocks their starch. Be sure to serve after a sugar-blocking first course.

Prep time: 10 minutes
Total time: 40 minutes
Makes 4 servings

2   sweet potatoes (about 1 pound), cut into 1"-thick slices
3   tablespoons butter, melted
¼   teaspoon salt
⅛   teaspoon ground black pepper

1. Preheat the oven to 375°F. In a large roasting pan, combine the sweet potatoes, butter, salt, and pepper. Toss to coat well.

2. Roast for 25 to 30 minutes, stirring occasionally, or until the sweet potatoes are tender and lightly browned.

Per serving: 174 calories ▶ 2 g protein ▶ 23 g carbohydrates ▶ 9 g fat ▶ 5.5 g saturated fat ▶ 3 g fiber ▶ 209 mg sodium

HALF-AND-HALF POTATO SALAD

Like potatoes, jicamas can be steamed, baked, boiled, mashed, or fried. Unlike potatoes, however, they can also be eaten raw. Crunchy pickles add flavor and texture to this salad, along with leveling out the glucose.

Prep time: 15 minutes
Total time: 40 minutes
Makes 6 servings

1   pound red potatoes, cut into ³/₄" pieces
1   small jicama (about 1 pound), peeled, halved, and cut into ½" pieces
¼   cup reduced-fat mayonnaise
¼   cup 2% plain Greek yogurt
3   tablespoons distilled white vinegar
1   tablespoon Dijon mustard
½   teaspoon stevia
½   teaspoon salt
¼   cup chopped reduced-sodium dill pickles
2   ribs celery, chopped
3   scallions, chopped

1. In a large saucepan, combine the potatoes, jicama, and enough cold water to cover by 3". Bring to a boil over high heat. Reduce the heat to medium, cover, and simmer for 20 minutes, or until tender. Drain and let cool.

2. In a large bowl, whisk together the mayonnaise, yogurt, vinegar, mustard, stevia, and salt until blended. Add the pickles, celery, scallions, and the cooled potato mixture. Toss to coat well.

Per serving: 160 calories ▶ 4 g protein ▶ 29 g carbohydrates ▶ 4 g fat ▶ 0.5 g saturated fat ▶ 8 g fiber ▶ 354 mg sodium

SWEET POTATO–CARROT PANCAKES

Carrots act as a great starch mimic for sweet potatoes.

Prep time: 15 minutes
Total time: 40 minutes
Makes 6 servings (12 pancakes)

- 2 sweet potatoes (1 pound), peeled and shredded
- 2 carrots, shredded
- 2 scallions, chopped
- 1/3 cup whole wheat pastry flour
- 1 egg
- 1/2 teaspoon salt
- 1/4 teaspoon ground black pepper
- 3 tablespoons olive oil
- 1/3 cup unsweetened applesauce
- 1/4 cup light sour cream

1. Preheat the oven to 200°F.

2. In a large bowl, stir together the potatoes, carrots, scallions, flour, egg, salt, and pepper.

3. Heat 1 tablespoon of the oil in a large nonstick skillet over medium-low heat. For each pancake, drop 1/4 cup of the sweet potato mixture into the skillet, making 4 pancakes at a time, flattening each with a spatula to a 3" round. Cook for 8 minutes, or until golden brown, turning with a spatula halfway through the cooking. Place on a baking sheet in the oven to keep warm. Repeat twice with the remaining 1 tablespoon oil and sweet potato mixture.

4. Serve the pancakes topped with the applesauce and sour cream.

....

Per serving: 191 calories ► 4 g protein ► 25 g carbohydrates ► 9 g fat ► 2 g saturated fat ► 6 g fiber ► 268 mg sodium

PROVENÇAL VEGGIES

This is a great dish to make when summer vegetables are at their peak. Serve with skewers of grilled shrimp, or as a main-dish salad tossed with 2 cups of cooked whole wheat penne pasta.

Prep time: 15 minutes
Total time: 20 minutes
Makes 6 servings

- 1 tablespoon olive oil
- 1 small onion, chopped
- 1 red bell pepper, chopped
- 2 small zucchini, halved lengthwise and sliced crosswise
- ½ pint cherry tomatoes, halved
- ⅓ cup kalamata olives, pitted and halved
- ¼ teaspoon salt
- 2 tablespoons pesto

Warm the oil in a large nonstick skillet over medium-high heat. Cook the onion and bell pepper for 2 minutes, stirring frequently, or until softened. Add the zucchini and cook for 3 minutes, stirring occasionally, or until tender-crisp. Add the tomatoes, olives, and salt. Remove the skillet from the heat and stir in the pesto.

Per serving: 124 calories ▶ 3 g protein ▶ 9 g carbohydrates ▶ 9 g fat ▶ 2 g saturated fat ▶ 2 g fiber ▶ 452 mg sodium

INDIAN-SPICED BROCCOLI AND CAULIFLOWER

Combining the fats of coconut milk and canola oil and not overcooking the broccoli and cauliflower are sugar-blocking techniques.

Prep time: 15 minutes
Total time: 20 minutes
Makes 4 servings

1 tablespoon canola oil
2 cloves garlic, minced
½ teaspoon ground cumin
½ teaspoon curry powder
¼ teaspoon salt
¼ teaspoon ground black pepper
3 cups broccoli florets
2 cups cauliflower florets
½ cup water
½ cup coconut milk
¼ cup chopped fresh cilantro

1. Warm the oil in a large nonstick skillet over medium heat. Cook the garlic, cumin, curry powder, salt, and pepper for 1 minute, stirring constantly, or until fragrant. Add the broccoli, cauliflower, and water. Increase the heat to medium-high and cook for 3 minutes, stirring frequently, or until the broccoli and cauliflower are tender-crisp and the liquid has evaporated.

2. Reduce the heat to medium. Stir in the coconut milk and simmer for 1 minute. Remove from the heat and stir in the cilantro.

Per serving: 120 calories ▶ 3 g protein ▶ 7 g carbohydrates ▶ 10 g fat ▶ 6 g saturated fat ▶ 3 g fiber ▶ 181 mg sodium

VINEGAR-GLAZED CARROTS

Two vinegars are used here: balsamic for a touch of sweetness, red wine vinegar for a bit of pucker.

Prep time: 10 minutes
Total time: 25 minutes
Makes 4 servings

1   tablespoon olive oil
6   carrots (about 1 pound), thinly sliced
1   shallot, finely chopped
2   tablespoons red wine vinegar
1   tablespoon balsamic vinegar
1   tablespoon butter
¼   teaspoon salt

Warm the oil in a large nonstick skillet over medium-high heat. Cook the carrots for 5 minutes, stirring occasionally, or until lightly browned. Add the shallot and cook for 2 minutes, or until soft. Add the red wine vinegar, balsamic vinegar, butter, and salt. Reduce the heat to medium and cook for 5 minutes, stirring occasionally, or until the carrots are tender-crisp and nicely glazed.

Per serving: 120 calories ▸ 2 g protein ▸ 15 g carbohydrates ▸ 7 g fat ▸ 2.5 g saturated fat ▸ 3 g fiber ▸ 225 mg sodium

SWISS CHARD WITH ALMONDS

When available, use colorful rainbow chard, as it is a tastier variety. Each type of chard—red, green, and rainbow—has a slightly different flavor.

Prep time: 10 minutes
Total time: 20 minutes
Makes 4 servings

- 2 tablespoons olive oil
- 1 small onion, halved and thinly sliced
- 3 cloves garlic, thinly sliced
- 1 bunch Swiss chard, coarsely chopped
- ¼ teaspoon salt
- ¼ cup sliced almonds, toasted

Warm the oil in a large nonstick skillet over medium-high heat. Cook the onion and garlic for 3 minutes, stirring occasionally, or until softened. Add the Swiss chard. Sprinkle with the salt and cook for 3 minutes, stirring occasionally, or until the chard is wilted. Serve sprinkled with the almonds.

Per serving: 152 calories ▶ 5 g protein ▶ 11 g carbohydrates ▶ 12 g fat ▶ 1.5 g saturated fat ▶ 4 g fiber ▶ 449 mg sodium

THREE-PEA SAUTÉ

For an Asian flare, toss the pea mixture with 1 teaspoon toasted sesame oil at the end of cooking time and sprinkle with 1 teaspoon toasted sesame seeds.

Prep time: 5 minutes
Total time: 10 minutes
Makes 4 servings

1 tablespoon canola oil
2 teaspoons finely chopped fresh ginger
1 clove garlic, minced
¼ pound snow peas
¼ pound sugar snap peas, strings removed
1 cup frozen green peas, thawed
¼ cup water
¼ teaspoon salt

Warm the oil in a large nonstick skillet over medium-high heat. Cook the ginger and garlic for 30 seconds, stirring constantly, or until fragrant. Add the snow peas, sugar snaps, frozen peas, water, and salt. Cook for 3 minutes, stirring occasionally, or until the liquid has evaporated and the peas are tender-crisp.

Per serving: 83 calories ▸ 3 g protein ▸ 9 g carbohydrates ▸ 4 g fat ▸ 0.5 g saturated fat ▸ 3 g fiber ▸ 186 mg sodium

TOMATOES WITH MOZZARELLA CHEESE

This works best with firm-ripe tomatoes. To make this into a main dish, serve the tomatoes over grilled chicken breasts, and be sure to spoon any juices from the skillet over the top.

Prep time: 10 minutes
Total time: 15 minutes
Makes 4 servings

- 2   tablespoons olive oil
- 1   clove garlic, minced
- 2   beefsteak tomatoes, each cut into 4 slices
- $\frac{1}{4}$ teaspoon salt
- $\frac{1}{8}$ teaspoon ground black pepper
- 16   fresh basil leaves
- 4   ounces fresh mozzarella cheese, cut into 8 slices

Warm the oil in a large nonstick skillet over medium-high heat. Cook the garlic for 2 minutes, stirring frequently, or until fragrant. Add the tomatoes in one layer, sprinkle with the salt and pepper, and cook for 1 minute, turning occasionally, or until softened. Scatter the basil over the tomato slices and top with the cheese. Cover and cook, without turning, for 1 minute, or until the cheese just begins to melt.

Per serving: 164 calories ▶ 6 g protein ▶ 5 g carbohydrates ▶ 13 g fat ▶ 5 g saturated fat ▶ 1 g fiber ▶ 243 mg sodium

CREAMED SPINACH

If you like, substitute 2 packages (10 ounces each) of frozen leaf spinach, thawed and squeezed dry, for the fresh spinach.

Prep time: 10 minutes
Total time: 20 minutes
Makes 4 servings

- 2 teaspoons olive oil
- 1 onion, chopped
- 1 clove garlic, minced
- 1 pound baby spinach
- 2 ounces reduced-fat cream cheese, at room temperature
- ¼ teaspoon salt
- ⅛ teaspoon ground black pepper
- ⅛ teaspoon ground nutmeg

Warm the oil in a large nonstick skillet over medium-high heat. Cook the onion and garlic for 5 minutes, stirring occasionally, or until softened. Add the spinach and cook for 2 to 3 minutes, stirring, or just until wilted. Stir in the cream cheese, salt, pepper, and nutmeg and cook for 1 minute, or until melted.

Per serving: 119 calories ▸ 4 g protein ▸ 16 g carbohydrates ▸ 6 g fat ▸ 2 g saturated fat ▸ 6 g fiber ▸ 374 mg sodium

ROASTED BROCCOLI WITH ORANGES

For added color and crunch, add a chopped yellow or orange bell pepper during the last 5 minutes of roasting time.

Prep time: 15 minutes
Total time: 40 minutes
Makes 4 servings

3   broccoli crowns (1½ pounds total), broken into florets
3   shallots, sliced
2   tablespoons olive oil
1   orange, peeled and cut crosswise into ½"-thick slices
1   tablespoon white wine vinegar
¼   teaspoon salt
¼   teaspoon ground black pepper

1. Preheat the oven to 425°F. In a large roasting pan, toss the broccoli, shallots, and oil until well coated. Spread in a single layer and roast for 15 minutes.

2. Tuck the orange slices into the broccoli and roast for 10 minutes, or until the oranges are softened and the broccoli is tender-crisp. Toss with the vinegar and sprinkle with the salt and pepper.

Per serving: 163 calories ▶ 7 g protein ▶ 23 g carbohydrates ▶ 8 g fat ▶ 1 g saturated fat ▶ 6 g fiber ▶ 191 mg sodium

BUTTERNUT AGRODOLCE

Agrodolce is a classic sweet-and-sour sauce used in many Italian dishes. Its name comes from *agro,* meaning "sour," and *dolce,* meaning "sweet."

Prep time: 10 minutes
Total time: 30 minutes
Makes 4 servings

1　tablespoon olive oil
2　cups frozen pearl onions
1　package (20 ounces) peeled butternut squash, cut into ¾" pieces
2　tablespoons red wine vinegar
2　tablespoons Sucanat
¼　teaspoon dried thyme
¼　teaspoon salt
¼　teaspoon ground black pepper
3　tablespoons pine nuts, toasted
2　tablespoons chopped fresh chives

1. Warm the oil in a large nonstick skillet over medium heat. Cook the pearl onions for 5 minutes, stirring occasionally, or until softened and lightly browned. Add the squash and 3 tablespoons water. Reduce the heat to low, cover, and cook for 10 minutes, or until the squash is almost tender.

2. In a cup, whisk together the vinegar, Sucanat, thyme, salt, and pepper. Drizzle over the squash and cook for 5 minutes over medium heat, stirring gently, or until the squash is fork-tender and flavored throughout.

3. Serve sprinkled with the pine nuts and chives.

Per serving: 216 calories ▶ 4 g protein ▶ 37 g carbohydrates ▶ 8 g fat
▶ 1 g saturated fat ▶ 5 g fiber ▶ 301 mg sodium

ASPARAGUS WITH SHALLOT DRESSING

Here's a perfect make-ahead dish. Refrigerate the cooked asparagus and vinaigrette separately and assemble right before serving.

Prep time: 10 minutes
Total time: 15 minutes
Makes 4 servings

- 2 tablespoons red wine vinegar
- 2 tablespoons + 1½ teaspoons olive oil
- 1 shallot, finely chopped
- 1 teaspoon Dijon mustard
- ¼ teaspoon dried tarragon
- ¼ teaspoon salt
- ¼ teaspoon ground black pepper
- 1½ pounds asparagus

1. In a small bowl, whisk together the vinegar, 2 tablespoons of the oil, the shallot, mustard, tarragon, salt, and pepper until blended.

2. Heat the remaining 1½ teaspoons oil in a large nonstick skillet over medium-high heat. Add the asparagus in one layer and cook for 5 minutes, shaking the pan to turn the asparagus, or until tender-crisp.

3. Transfer to a serving platter and drizzle with the vinaigrette.

Per serving: 126 calories ▶ 4 g protein ▶ 10 g carbohydrates ▶ 9 g fat ▶ 1 g saturated fat ▶ 4 g fiber ▶ 179 mg sodium

ROASTED FENNEL AND SWEET ONIONS

Super quick and easy (and no dishes to clean), this is
the perfect side dish. Pop it in the oven along with
some oven-roasted fish fillets for a fuss-free meal.

Prep time: 10 minutes
Total time: 35 minutes
Makes 4 servings

1   large bulb fennel (1½ pounds), stalks discarded,
     bulb halved lengthwise and thinly sliced
½   large sweet onion, thinly sliced
1½ tablespoons olive oil
1   tablespoon distilled white vinegar
½   teaspoon crushed fennel seeds
½   teaspoon salt
¼   teaspoon ground black pepper

Preheat the oven to 425°F. In a large roasting pan, toss the fennel, onion, oil, vinegar,
fennel seeds, salt, and pepper until well coated. Spread evenly in the pan. Cover with foil
and roast for 15 minutes. Remove the foil and roast for 10 minutes, stirring occasionally,
or until tender.

Per serving: 143 calories ► 3 g protein ► 23 g carbohydrates ► 6 g fat
► 1 g saturated fat ► 7 g fiber ► 384 mg sodium

STIR-FRIED BOK CHOY

You can use baby bok choy instead of the larger bunch. Since they are small, you don't need to cut them into slices. Halve them lengthwise, place them cut side down in the skillet, and proceed with step 2.

Prep time: 10 minutes
Total time: 20 minutes
Makes 4 servings

---

2   teaspoons canola oil
2   cloves garlic, minced
1   teaspoon finely chopped fresh ginger
2   pounds bok choy, cut into ¼"-wide slices
1   tablespoon rice wine vinegar
2   teaspoons reduced-sodium soy sauce
1   teaspoon toasted sesame oil
2-3 drops hot-pepper sauce

1. Heat the canola oil in a large nonstick skillet over medium-high heat. Cook the garlic and ginger for 1 minute, stirring, or until fragrant.

2. Add the bok choy, vinegar, soy sauce, sesame oil, and hot-pepper sauce. Cover and cook for 3 minutes, or until the bok choy begins to wilt. Uncover and cook for 2 minutes, stirring frequently, or until the bok choy is tender-crisp.

Per serving: 70 calories ▶ 3 g protein ▶ 5 g carbohydrates ▶ 4 g fat ▶ 0 g saturated fat ▶ 2 g fiber ▶ 350 mg sodium

GREEN BEANS AMANDINE

Because nuts are added to the beans in this classic
dish, it's perfect for sugar blocking.

Prep time: 10 minutes
Total time: 25 minutes
Makes 4 servings

---

1   pound green beans, cut into 2" pieces
1   tablespoon unsalted butter
¼   cup slivered almonds
⅛   teaspoon salt
⅛   teaspoon ground black pepper

1. In a large skillet, bring 3" of water to a boil over high heat. Add the beans, reduce the
   heat to medium, cover, and simmer for 5 minutes, or until the beans are tender-crisp.
   Drain well.

2. In the same skillet, heat the butter over medium heat. Cook the almonds for 2 to
   3 minutes, stirring frequently, or until the almonds are lightly browned. Add the
   beans, salt, and pepper and cook for 1 minute, stirring, or until heated through.

Per serving: 100 calories ▸ 4 g protein ▸ 10 g carbohydrates ▸ 6 g fat
▸ 2 g saturated fat ▸ 5 g fiber ▸ 85 mg sodium

DESSERTS

CHERRY-GINGER APPLESAUCE

Try substituting firm-ripe pears for the apples. If you prefer a fine-textured applesauce, puree it using a hand-held blender or mini food processor.

Prep time: 15 minutes
Total time: 45 minutes
Makes 4 servings

4   large apples, peeled and cut into 1" pieces
3   tablespoons dried cherries, finely chopped
1   teaspoon grated fresh ginger
½   teaspoon ground cinnamon
1   packet stevia
⅓   cup water

1. In a large saucepan, combine the apples, cherries, ginger, cinnamon, stevia, and water. Bring to a boil over high heat. Reduce the heat to medium, cover, and simmer for 15 minutes, or until the apples are fork-tender.

2. Mash with a potato masher or a fork and cook, uncovered, for 5 to 10 minutes, or until thick.

Per serving: 128 calories ▸ 1 g protein ▸ 33 g carbohydrates ▸ 0 g fat ▸ 0 g saturated fat ▸ 4 g fiber ▸ 3 mg sodium

CHOCOLATE-PISTACHIO-DIPPED APRICOTS

Chopped almonds can be used in place of the pistachios. Store the apricots in an airtight container in the refrigerator for up to 2 weeks.

Prep time: 15 minutes
Total time: 20 minutes
Makes 12 servings

---

2   ounces bittersweet or semisweet chocolate, chopped (¼ cup)
1½ tablespoons finely chopped pistachios
24 dried apricots (4 ounces)

Place the chocolate in a small microwaveable cup. Microwave on high power for 30 to 40 seconds, stirring, or until melted and smooth. Place the pistachios on a sheet of waxed paper and line a plate with waxed paper. Dip each apricot into the melted chocolate to coat about two-thirds of the apricot. Dip lightly, coated end down, into the pistachios and place on the lined plate.

Per serving: 51 calories ▶ 1 g protein ▶ 7 g carbohydrates ▶ 2 g fat
▶ 1 g saturated fat ▶ 1 g fiber ▶ 2 mg sodium

GINGER PEAR CRISP

If you like, serve the crisp topped with plain Greek yogurt.

Prep time: 15 minutes
Total time: 40 minutes
Makes 6 servings

4   large pears (2 pounds), peeled and sliced
2   teaspoons grated fresh ginger
¼   cup Sucanat, divided
¾   cup old-fashioned rolled oats
¼   cup almond or coconut flour
2   tablespoons ground flaxseed
3   tablespoons butter, melted
4   packets stevia
½   teaspoon pumpkin pie spice
⅛   teaspoon salt

1. Preheat the oven to 400°F. Coat a 2-quart baking dish with cooking spray. Add the pears, ginger, and 2 tablespoons of the Sucanat to the dish and toss to coat.

2. In a medium bowl, combine the oats, almond flour, flaxseed, butter, stevia, pumpkin pie spice, salt, and the remaining 2 tablespoons Sucanat. Rub the mixture together with your fingers until it resembles coarse crumbs and begins to form clumps when squeezed.

3. Sprinkle the oat mixture over the pear mixture to cover. Bake for 25 minutes, or until the filling is hot and bubbling and the top is lightly golden.

Per serving: 254 calories ▸ 4 g protein ▸ 40 g carbohydrates ▸ 10 g fat ▸ 4 g saturated fat ▸ 7 g fiber ▸ 57 mg sodium

STRAWBERRY-RHUBARB SLUMP

A slump is an old-fashioned dessert topped with a biscuitlike dough. Instead of baking in the oven, it is cooked on top of the stove. If fresh rhubarb is unavailable, use 4 cups frozen cut rhubarb, thawed.

Prep time: 15 minutes
Total time: 40 minutes
Makes 8 servings

Filling
- ⅓ cup Sucanat
- 3 tablespoons spoonable stevia
- 1½ tablespoons arrowroot
- ¾ teaspoon pumpkin pie spice
- ½ cup water
- 1 pound rhubarb, cut into 1" pieces
- 4 cups strawberries, quartered lengthwise

Dumplings
- ¾ cup whole grain pastry flour
- ⅓ cup almond or coconut flour
- 2 tablespoons Sucanat
- 1¼ teaspoons baking powder
- ¼ teaspoon baking soda
- ⅛ teaspoon salt
- 3 tablespoons cold butter, cut into small pieces
- ½ cup buttermilk

1. *To make the filling:* In a large, deep skillet, combine the Sucanat, stevia, arrowroot, pie spice, and water and stir to blend. Stir in the rhubarb and strawberries. Bring to a boil over medium-high heat and boil for 2 minutes, or until the mixture thickens and turns clear. Remove from the heat. Set aside.

2. *To make the dumplings:* In a food processor, combine the pastry flour, almond flour, Sucanat, baking powder, baking soda, and salt and process to blend. Add the butter and pulse until the mixture resembles fine crumbs. Add the buttermilk and pulse until a soft dough forms.

3. Drop large spoonfuls of the dough over the fruit mixture, spacing them so that they don't touch each other. Cover with a lid or foil. Cook over medium-low heat for 20 to 25 minutes, or until the fruit is tender and the dumplings are firm to the touch. Let cool, uncovered, for 10 minutes before serving.

Per serving: 202 calories ▸ 4 g protein ▸ 32 g carbohydrates ▸ 7 g fat ▸ 3 g saturated fat ▸ 5 g fiber ▸ 180 mg sodium

ROAST PEACHES WITH STREUSEL TOPPING

Almond flour, also known as almond meal, can be found in health food stores and in the natural foods section of most supermarkets.

Prep time: 10 minutes
Total time: 40 minutes
Makes 4 servings

4   peaches, halved and pitted
3   tablespoons butter, at room temperature
3   tablespoons Sucanat
1½ teaspoons spoonable stevia
½   teaspoon ground cinnamon
⅓   cup almond flour
3   tablespoons chopped pecans

1. Preheat the oven to 375°F. Coat a 13" × 9" baking dish with cooking spray. Place the peach halves cut side up in the dish.

2. In a medium bowl, beat together the butter, Sucanat, stevia, and cinnamon until blended. Let stand for 5 minutes. Stir in the almond flour and pecans. Rub the mixture together with your fingers until it resembles coarse crumbs.

3. Sprinkle the crumb mixture over the peaches and bake for 30 minutes, or until the peaches are tender and the top is lightly golden.

Per serving: 258 calories ▶ 4 g protein ▶ 27 g carbohydrates ▶ 17 g fat ▶ 6 g saturated fat ▶ 4 g fiber ▶ 10 mg sodium

GRAPES WITH SOUR CREAM

Use this delicious sour cream topping for other fruits such as strawberries, peaches, or nectarines.

Prep time: 15 minutes
Total time: 15 minutes
Makes 4 servings

- ¼ cup sour cream
- ¼ cup 0% plain Greek yogurt
- 1 tablespoon Sucanat
- 1 cup seedless red grapes, halved
- 1 cup seedless green grapes, halved
- ½ teaspoon spoonable stevia
- ½ teaspoon grated orange peel

1. In a small bowl, mix together the sour cream, yogurt, and Sucanat. Let stand for 10 minutes, or until the Sucanat is dissolved.

2. In a medium bowl, combine the red grapes, green grapes, stevia, and orange peel and toss to coat.

3. Serve the grape mixture dolloped with the sour cream mixture.

Per serving: 95 calories ▶ 2 g protein ▶ 18 g carbohydrates ▶ 2 g fat ▶ 1.5 g saturated fat ▶ 1 g fiber ▶ 18 mg sodium

FRESH FRUIT TART

The tart can be made ahead of time and refrigerated, covered, for up to 8 hours or overnight.

Prep time: 20 minutes
Total time: 1 hour 5 minutes
Makes 10 servings

1   cup whole grain pastry flour
⅓   cup almond flour
¼   cup Sucanat
8   tablespoons (1 stick) cold butter, cut into small pieces
1   egg yolk
½   cup cold heavy cream
8   ounces cream cheese, at room temperature
1   tablespoon spoonable stevia
⅛   teaspoon almond extract
1   kiwifruit, peeled, halved lengthwise, and sliced crosswise
1   cup sliced strawberries
1   cup raspberries
3   tablespoons apricot all-fruit spread, melted

1. In a food processor, combine the pastry flour, almond flour, and Sucanat and process to blend. Add the butter and pulse until the mixture resembles fine crumbs. Add the egg yolk and pulse until a soft dough forms. Gather the mixture into a ball and press into a thick disk. Cover and refrigerate for 15 minutes.

2. Preheat the oven to 375°F.

3. On a lightly floured surface, roll out the dough into an 11" round. Transfer the dough to a 9" tart pan with a removable bottom. Firmly press the dough against the bottom and sides of the pan. Trim the edges. Prick the bottom of the dough all over with a fork. Line with foil or parchment paper and weight down with pie weights or dried beans. Bake for 15 minutes. Remove the foil and weights. Bake for 5 minutes longer, or until lightly browned. Cool completely on a rack.

4. Meanwhile, in a medium bowl, with an electric mixer on medium-high speed, beat the heavy cream until stiff peaks form. In a large bowl, stir together the cream cheese, stevia, and almond extract until blended. With a rubber spatula, gently fold in the whipped cream until well combined.

5. Spread the filling evenly into the cooled tart shell. Arrange the fruit over the filling. Brush the fruit with the apricot fruit spread.

Per serving: 258 calories ▶ 3 g protein ▶ 20 g carbohydrates ▶ 20 g fat ▶ 11.5 g saturated fat ▶ 3 g fiber ▶ 16 mg sodium

KEY LIME PIE

Ground flaxseed and almond flour not only add fiber to the crust, but also help to block the sugar in this recipe. If you prefer to use prepared graham cracker crumbs, you will need 1 cup for the crust.

Prep time: 15 minutes
Total time: 30 minutes + chilling time
Makes 10 servings

8   full graham cracker sheets, coarsely crushed
⅓   cup almond flour
3   tablespoons ground flaxseeds
4   tablespoons unsalted butter, at room temperature
1   package (4-serving size) sugar-free lime gelatin
½   cup boiling water
4   ounces reduced-fat cream cheese, at room temperature
2   cups 2% plain Greek yogurt
1   teaspoon grated lime peel
2   tablespoons fresh lime juice

1. In a food processor, process the graham crackers until fine crumbs form. Add the almond flour and flaxseeds and pulse until blended. Add the butter and pulse just until the mixture resembles coarse crumbs. Press the mixture into the bottom and up the sides of a 9" pie plate.

2. In a medium bowl, whisk together the gelatin and boiling water until the gelatin completely dissolves. Whisk in the cream cheese until blended and smooth. Stir in the yogurt, lime peel, and lime juice until well mixed.

3. Spread the filling into the crust. Refrigerate for at least 1 hour before cutting into 10 slices.

Per serving: 171 calories ▶ 7 g protein ▶ 12 g carbohydrates ▶ 11 g fat ▶ 5 g saturated fat ▶ 1 g fiber ▶ 130 mg sodium

CHOCOLATE BANANA BREAD

This rich chocolate bread is great to keep on hand in the freezer. For optimum sugar blocking, choose a banana that is a little underripe, with some green in the skin, and free of any brown spots.

Prep time: 20 minutes
Total time: 1 hour 15 minutes
Makes 12 servings

½ cup low-fat plain yogurt
½ cup Sucanat
1 tablespoon instant espresso powder
½ cup mashed banana (about 1 small)
⅓ cup canola oil
1 egg
3 tablespoons spoonable stevia
2 teaspoons vanilla extract
1¼ cups whole grain pastry flour
½ cup unsweetened cocoa powder
½ cup unsweetened shredded coconut
¾ teaspoon baking powder
½ teaspoon baking soda
¼ teaspoon salt

1. Preheat the oven to 350°F. Coat an 8" × 4" loaf pan with cooking spray.

2. In a large bowl, whisk together the yogurt, Sucanat, and espresso powder until blended. Let stand for 5 minutes, or until the Sucanat is dissolved. Stir in the banana, oil, egg, stevia, and vanilla until well mixed.

3. In a small bowl, combine the flour, cocoa powder, coconut, baking powder, baking soda, and salt until blended. Stir into the yogurt mixture just until combined. Scrape the batter into the pan, smoothing the top with a rubber spatula.

4. Bake for 45 to 50 minutes, or until a wooden pick inserted in the center comes out clean. Cool for 10 minutes in the pan on a rack. Remove to the rack and cool completely.

Per serving: 165 calories ▶ 3 g protein ▶ 22 g carbohydrates ▶ 8 g fat ▶ 2 g saturated fat ▶ 2 g fiber ▶ 148 mg sodium

MINI CRANBERRY-LEMON LOAVES

These loaves freeze well; wrapped tightly in foil they'll keep for up to 2 months.

Prep time: 20 minutes
Total time: 55 minutes
Makes 12 servings

²/₃ cup buttermilk
½ cup Sucanat
3 tablespoons butter, melted
1 egg, lightly beaten
1 teaspoon grated lemon peel
1½ cups whole grain pastry flour
½ cup unsweetened shredded coconut
1½ tablespoons spoonable stevia
2 teaspoons baking powder
¼ teaspoon baking soda
½ teaspoon salt
1 cup fresh or frozen cranberries, coarsely chopped
⅓ cup dried cranberries
½ cup chopped walnuts

1. Preheat the oven to 375°F. Coat three 6" × 3" mini-loaf pans with cooking spray.

2. In a large bowl, whisk together the buttermilk and Sucanat. Let stand for at least 5 minutes, or until the Sucanat is dissolved. Stir in the butter, egg, and lemon peel until combined. In a small bowl, stir together the flour, coconut, stevia, baking powder, baking soda, and salt until blended. Add to the buttermilk mixture in 2 additions, until almost combined. Stir in the fresh (or frozen) cranberries, dried cranberries, and walnuts. Divide the batter among the loaf pans, smoothing the tops with a rubber spatula.

3. Bake for 35 minutes, or until a wooden pick inserted in the center of a loaf comes out clean. Cool for 10 minutes in the pans on a rack. Remove to the rack and cool completely.

Per serving: 177 calories ▶ 3 g protein ▶ 25 g carbohydrates ▶ 8 g fat ▶ 3 g saturated fat ▶ 3 g fiber ▶ 229 mg sodium

CAPPUCCINO MUFFINS

Using almond flour for a portion of the flour is the perfect way to block the starch in these muffins.

Prep time: 15 minutes
Total time: 40 minutes
Makes 12

Muffins

1¾ cups whole grain pastry flour
¾ cup almond flour
12 packets stevia
2 teaspoons baking powder
¾ teaspoon ground cinnamon
½ teaspoon baking soda
½ teaspoon salt
1 cup buttermilk
1 egg
3 tablespoons coconut oil or canola
1½ teaspoons instant espresso powder

Cream Cheese Icing

2 tablespoons reduced-fat cream cheese, at room temperature
1 packet stevia
¼ teaspoon fresh lemon juice
   Pinch of ground cinnamon

1. Preheat the oven to 350°F. Line a 12-cup muffin pan with paper liners or coat with cooking spray.

2. *To make the muffins:* In a large bowl, whisk together the pastry flour, almond flour, stevia, baking powder, cinnamon, baking soda, and salt. In a small bowl, beat together the buttermilk, egg, oil, and espresso powder until blended. Add to the flour mixture and stir just until moistened.

3. Divide the batter among the muffin cups. Bake for 15 to 20 minutes, or until a wooden pick inserted in the center of a muffin comes out clean. Cool in the pan on a rack for 5 minutes. Remove to the rack and cool completely.

4. *Meanwhile, to make the icing:* In a small bowl, combine the cream cheese, stevia, lemon juice, and cinnamon until blended. Drizzle over the cooled muffins.

....

Per muffin: 163 calories ▶ 4 g protein ▶ 18 g carbohydrates ▶ 9 g fat
▶ 4 g saturated fat ▶ 3 g fiber ▶ 275 mg sodium

RASPBERRY FOOL

Keep the heavy cream in the refrigerator until just before beating for maximum volume. When pureeing raspberries, frozen are more economical to use, and frequently they have more flavor, since they are frozen at their peak.

Prep time: 20 minutes
Total time: 30 minutes
Makes 4 servings

1   package (12 ounces) frozen raspberries, thawed
¼   cup Sucanat
½   cup plain Greek yogurt
¾   cup heavy cream
¼   teaspoon vanilla extract
½   cup fresh raspberries
2   tablespoons sliced almonds, toasted

1. In a food processor, pulse the raspberries until smooth. With the back of a large spoon, press the mixture through a fine sieve over a medium bowl to remove the seeds. Add the Sucanat to the puree and let stand for 5 minutes, or until the Sucanat is completely dissolved. Stir in the yogurt until blended.

2. Meanwhile, in a medium bowl, with an electric mixer on high speed, beat the cream and vanilla until stiff peaks form. Fold into the raspberry mixture.

3. Serve the raspberry mixture topped with the fresh raspberries and almonds.

Per serving: 298 calories ▶ 4 g protein ▶ 23 g carbohydrates ▶ 22 g fat ▶ 13 g saturated fat ▶ 4 g fiber ▶ 33 mg sodium

LAYERED CHOCOLATE PUDDING

Sugar-free pudding mix creates a luscious dessert treat with minimal carbs. Be sure to eat this after a very low-carb meal with plenty of sugar blockers such as meat, cheese, vinegar, and nuts.

Prep time: 30 minutes
Total time: 50 minutes
Makes 8 servings

- 4 sugar-free sandwich cookies
- 1 (1 ounce) package instant sugar-free, fat-free white chocolate pudding mix
- 4 cups whole milk, divided
- 1 (1.4 ounces) package instant sugar-free, fat-free chocolate pudding mix
- 4 tablespoons sugar-free hot fudge topping
- 1 cup heavy cream, whipped
  Chocolate curls and/or cocoa powder for garnish

1. Place the cookies in a ziptop plastic bag and seal. Crush with a rolling pin. Divide among 8 custard cups, ramekins, or small dessert dishes.

2. In a medium bowl, prepare the white chocolate pudding mix with 2 cups milk according to package directions. Let set for 10 minutes. In another medium bowl, prepare the chocolate pudding mix with 2 cups milk according to package directions. Let set for 10 minutes.

3. Divide the white chocolate pudding among the dishes and form a layer. Divide the chocolate pudding over the white chocolate pudding. Refrigerate until ready to serve.

4. To serve, top each dish with ½ tablespoon hot fudge topping and 2 tablespoons whipped cream. Garnish if desired.

Per serving: 255 calories ▸ 5 g protein ▸ 23 g carbohydrates ▸ 16 g fat ▸ 9.5 g saturated fat ▸ 1 g fiber ▸ 404 mg sodium

CHOCOLATE POTS DE CRÈME

Pots de crème is French for "pots of cream," a term that refers both to the custard and to the small lidded pots they are traditionally baked in. To make a mocha version, add 1 teaspoon instant espresso powder to the custard in step 2 with the chocolate.

Prep time: 15 minutes
Total time: 40 minutes + chilling time
Makes 4 servings

1   cup half-and-half
¼   cup Sucanat
4   ounces bittersweet chocolate, finely chopped
½   teaspoon vanilla extract
2   eggs

1. Preheat the oven to 325°F. Bring a kettle of water to a boil.

2. In a medium saucepan over medium heat, combine the half-and-half and Sucanat and bring just to a boil. Remove from the heat and stir in the chocolate and vanilla, whisking until the chocolate is melted and the mixture is smooth.

3. In a medium bowl, lightly beat the eggs. Whisk in the chocolate mixture in a slow, steady stream, whisking constantly.

4. Divide the custard evenly among four 6-ounce ramekins or custard cups and place in a shallow roasting pan. Put the pan on a pulled-out oven rack and add enough boiling water to the pan to come halfway up the sides of the ramekins. Loosely cover the pan with foil (to prevent a skin from forming on the custards) and bake for 25 minutes, or until the custards are barely set around the edges and jiggle in the center. Do not overbake. The custards will continue to firm up as they cool.

5. Carefully transfer the ramekins to a rack to cool. Refrigerate, covered, for 3 hours or up to 1 day, until thoroughly chilled and set.

Per serving: 316 calories ▸ 7 g protein ▸ 28 g carbohydrates ▸ 21 g fat
▸ 11.5 g saturated fat ▸ 3 g fiber ▸ 71 mg sodium

ROASTED PINEAPPLE SUNDAES

Unsweetened coconut can be found in most super-markets or in health food stores. It comes finely shred-ded or in larger shards. Either will work here.

Prep time: 15 minutes
Total time: 40 minutes +
cooling time
Makes 4 servings

1   tablespoon butter, at room temperature
4   slices (¾") fresh pineapple (about ¼ medium pineapple)
3   tablespoons Sucanat, divided
½   cup heavy cream
¼   teaspoon vanilla extract
2   cups sugar-free vanilla ice cream
¼   cup salted macadamia nuts, chopped
2   tablespoons unsweetened shredded coconut, toasted

1. Preheat the oven to 425°F. Spread the butter on the bottom of a shallow baking pan. Place the pineapple in the pan and sprinkle evenly with 1 tablespoon of the Sucanat. Bake for 20 minutes, turning once, or until tender and lightly browned.

2. In a small saucepan, combine the heavy cream and the remaining 2 tablespoons Sucanat and bring to a boil over medium-high heat. Reduce the heat to medium-low and cook for 5 minutes, stirring, or until the sauce bubbles and thickens. Remove from the heat and stir in the vanilla. Let the sauce cool for 10 minutes.

3. Place a pineapple slice on each of 4 plates. Top each with ½ cup ice cream. Drizzle with the vanilla sauce and sprinkle with the nuts and coconut.

Per serving: 353 calories ▸ 3 g protein ▸ 32 g carbohydrates ▸ 25 g fat ▸ 12.5 g saturated fat ▸ 2 g fiber ▸ 76 mg sodium

STRAWBERRY MALTED MILKSHAKE

You can leave out the malted milk powder if you prefer. Using this recipe as a guideline, get the family involved by creating their own favorite ice cream and fruit combinations.

Prep time: 10 minutes
Total time: 10 minutes
Makes 1 serving

½ cup sugar-free vanilla ice cream
1 cup strawberries, quartered
¼ cup cold whole milk
2 tablespoons malted milk powder

In a blender, combine the ice cream, strawberries, milk, and malted milk powder and blend until smooth. Pour into a tall glass and serve immediately.

Per serving: 214 calories ▸ 7 g protein ▸ 34 g carbohydrates ▸ 7 g fat ▸ 4 g saturated fat ▸ 4 g fiber ▸ 111 mg sodium

CHERRIES 'N' CHOCOLATE SUNDAES

Be sure to use premium ice cream in this dish; along with the nuts, it helps block the sugar. When cherries are in season, make this sauce with 2 cups of pitted and halved fresh cherries.

Prep time: 15 minutes
Total time: 15 minutes
Makes 6 servings

1   bag (12 ounces) frozen unsweetened dark cherries, thawed and drained
⅓   cup low-sugar cherry jam
2   teaspoons brandy or cognac (optional)
1   pint premium vanilla ice cream
2   ounces dark chocolate, chopped
¼   cup toasted pecans, coarsely chopped

1. In a medium bowl, combine the cherries, jam, and brandy until blended.

2. Divide half of the cherry mixture among 6 sundae dishes or bowls. Top each with ⅓ cup of the ice cream. Top with the remaining cherry mixture and sprinkle with the chocolate and pecans.

Per serving: 296 calories ▶ 4 g protein ▶ 35 g carbohydrates ▶ 16 g fat ▶ 9 g saturated fat ▶ 1 g fiber ▶ 33 mg sodium

NO-BAKE LEMON CHEESECAKE

The full-fat cream cheese and yogurt in this dessert make a deliciously rich treat and work as sugar blockers. You can make this in a 9" springform pan, also.

Prep time: 20 minutes
Total time: 3 hours 30 minutes
Makes 12 servings

14 graham cracker squares, crumbled (1 cup crumbs)
2 tablespoons ground flaxseed
3 tablespoons unsalted butter, melted
1 envelope unflavored gelatin
½ cup water
½ cup Sucanat
1¼ pounds cream cheese, at room temperature
1 cup whole-milk plain Greek yogurt
3 tablespoons spoonable stevia
2 teaspoons grated lemon peel
¼ cup fresh lemon juice
Sliced strawberries, for garnish

1. Line the bottom of an 8" × 8" baking pan with foil, extending the foil by 2" over two opposite sides.

2. In a food processor, pulse the graham crackers until finely ground. Add the flaxseed and butter and pulse until the mixture resembles coarse crumbs. Sprinkle the mixture into the pan, tilting the pan to lightly coat the sides and pressing the crumbs into the bottom of the pan.

3. In a small saucepan, sprinkle the gelatin over the water and let stand for 5 minutes to soften. Set the pan over low heat and cook for 1 to 2 minutes, stirring, or until the gelatin is dissolved. Remove from the heat and stir in the Sucanat. Let stand for 5 minutes, stirring occasionally, or until the Sucanat is completely dissolved.

4. Meanwhile, in a large bowl, with an electric mixer on medium speed, beat the cream cheese for 2 minutes, or until blended and smooth. Beat in the yogurt, stevia, lemon peel, lemon juice, and the gelatin mixture, beating for 1 minute, or until blended.

5. Pour the batter over the crust and smooth the top. Refrigerate, uncovered, for 3 hours, or until set.

6. To serve, using the foil overhang, lift the cheesecake onto a cutting board. Cut into 12 pieces. Serve with the strawberries.

Per serving: 291 calories ▶ 6 g protein ▶ 18 g carbohydrates ▶ 22 g fat ▶ 12.5 g saturated fat ▶ 1 g fiber ▶ 215 mg sodium

CHOCOLATE-NUT COOKIES

If you can't find oat flour in your supermarket or health food store, it's simple enough to make yourself. Place quick-cooking or rolled oats in a food processor and process until finely ground. You'll need about ⅔ cup of oats to make ½ cup oat flour.

Prep time: 15 minutes
Total time: 25 minutes
Makes 16

- 2 tablespoons unsalted butter, at room temperature
- 3 tablespoons spoonable stevia
- 1 egg
- 1 teaspoon vanilla extract
- ½ cup oat flour
- 2 tablespoons unsweetened cocoa powder
- ½ teaspoon baking powder
  Pinch of salt
- 1 cup chopped pecans
- 2 ounces bittersweet or semisweet chocolate, coarsely chopped

1. Preheat the oven to 350°F. Line a large baking sheet with parchment paper or coat with cooking spray.

2. In a large bowl, with an electric mixer on medium-high speed, beat the butter, stevia, egg, and vanilla until creamy. Reduce the speed to low and beat in the flour, cocoa powder, baking powder, and salt until blended. Fold in the pecans and chopped chocolate.

3. Roll the dough into 16 balls (1" diameter) and place 2" apart on the baking sheet. Flatten the cookies slightly. Bake for 10 minutes, or until lightly browned. Cool on the baking sheet for 2 minutes. Transfer to racks and cool completely.

....

Per cookie: 94 calories ▸ 2 g protein ▸ 7 g carbohydrates ▸ 8 g fat ▸ 2.5 g saturated fat ▸ 1 g fiber ▸ 40 mg sodium

NUTTY OATMEAL COOKIES

You can use other dried fruits, such as apricots or cherries, instead of the cranberries.

Prep time: 15 minutes

Total time: 30 minutes

Makes 24

4   tablespoons (½ stick) butter, at room temperature
½   cup Sucanat
2   tablespoons canola oil
2   teaspoons spoonable stevia
1   egg
1   teaspoon vanilla extract
¾   cup whole grain pastry flour
½   teaspoon baking soda
½   teaspoon ground cinnamon
¼   teaspoon salt
1   cup quick-cooking oats
⅓   cup dried cranberries, chopped
⅓   cup chopped pecans
⅓   cup chopped walnuts

1. Preheat the oven to 350°F. Coat 2 large baking sheets with cooking spray.

2. In a large bowl, with an electric mixer on medium-high speed, beat the butter, Sucanat, oil, stevia, egg, and vanilla until well blended. Reduce to low and beat in the flour, baking soda, cinnamon, and salt until blended. Stir in the oats, cranberries, pecans, and walnuts until well mixed.

3. Drop the dough by rounded tablespoons 2" apart onto the baking sheets. Flatten the cookies slightly. Bake for 12 minutes, or until the cookies are lightly browned around the edges. Cool on the baking sheets for 2 minutes. Transfer to racks and cool completely.

Per cookie: 90 calories ▸ 2 g protein ▸ 9 g carbohydrates ▸ 5 g fat ▸ 1.5 g saturated fat ▸ 1 g fiber ▸ 56 mg sodium

PEANUT BUTTER CHOCOLATE CHIP COOKIES

This recipe works well with either smooth or chunky peanut butter; just be sure to use natural peanut butter with no added sugar. The chia seeds not only help block much of the sugar, they also keep the cookies soft.

Prep time: 15 minutes
Total time: 30 minutes
Makes 24

2 tablespoons chia seeds
2 tablespoons water
¾ cup chunky natural peanut butter
6 tablespoons butter, at room temperature
⅓ cup Sucanat
2 tablespoons spoonable stevia
2 eggs
1 teaspoon vanilla extract
¾ cup whole grain pastry flour
¾ cup oat flour
¼ teaspoon baking soda
¼ teaspoon salt
½ cup bittersweet or semisweet chocolate chips

1. Preheat the oven to 350°F. Coat 2 large baking sheets with cooking spray. In a small bowl, combine the chia seeds and water and let stand for 10 minutes.

2. In a bowl, with an electric mixer, beat the peanut butter, butter, Sucanat, and stevia until smooth and creamy. Beat in the eggs, vanilla, and the chia seed mixture until well blended. On low speed, beat in the pastry flour, oat flour, baking soda, and salt until blended. Stir in the chocolate chips.

3. Roll the dough by level tablespoons into 24 balls, about 1¼" each and place 2" apart on the baking sheets. With the back of a fork, press down on the balls in a crisscross pattern. Bake for 12 minutes, or until lightly browned at the edges. Cool on the baking sheets for 2 minutes. Transfer to racks and cool completely.

Per cookie: 137 calories ▶ 4 g protein ▶ 11 g carbohydrates ▶ 9 g fat ▶ 3 g saturated fat ▶ 2 g fiber ▶ 76 mg sodium

ALMOND BUTTER SHORTBREAD COOKIES

The nut butter and nuts are the sugar blockers in these rich, delicious bites. Other nuts such as cashews and cashew butter would work well in this shortbread.

Prep time: 15 minutes
Total time: 40 minutes
Makes 24

1¼ cups whole wheat pastry flour
½ cup sliced almonds
½ cup Sucanat
½ cup almond butter
4 tablespoons (½ stick) cold unsalted butter, cut into small pieces
¼ teaspoon salt
½ teaspoon almond extract

1. Preheat the oven to 300°F. Line a large baking sheet with parchment paper.

2. In a food processor, combine the flour, almonds, and Sucanat and pulse until the almonds are finely ground. Add the almond butter, unsalted butter, salt, and almond extract. Pulse until the mixture is crumbly.

3. Turn the dough out onto a lightly floured surface and gather into a ball. Divide the dough in half. Knead each portion twice. Place the 2 pieces of dough on the baking sheet 8″ apart. Pat each piece of dough into a 6″ round. Crimp the edges. With a sharp knife, score each round into 12 wedges, cutting almost, but not quite through, to the bottom.

4. Bake for 25 minutes, or until crisp and lightly golden. Remove from the oven and while still warm, cut the wedges through to the bottom. Cool on the baking sheet on a rack.

....

Per cookie: 100 calories ▸ 2 g protein ▸ 10 g carbohydrates ▸ 6 g fat
▸ 1.5 g saturated fat ▸ 1 g fiber ▸ 50 mg sodium

INDEX